BESTSELLING NON-FICTION

- Annihilation of Caste by Dr B.R. Ambedkar
  Social Science, ISBN: 9789390492732
- Believe in Yourself by Joseph Murphy
  Self-Help/Motivational, ISBN: 9789388118385
- How I Made $2,000,000 in the Stock Market by Nicolas Darvas
  Self-Help, ISBN: 9789389716283
- How to Attract Money by Joseph Murphy
  Self-Help, ISBN: 9789388118408
- How to Enjoy Your Life and Your Job by Dale Carnegie
  Self-Help, ISBN: 9789387669017
- How to Stop Worrying and Start Living by Dale Carnegie
  Self-Help, ISBN: 9789380914817
- How to Win Friends and Influence People by Dale Carnegie
  Self-Help, ISBN: 9788180320217
- Jail Diary and Other Writings by Bhagat Singh
  Biographies & Memoirs, ISBN: 9789390492398
- Know Your Worth by NK Sondhi & Vibha Malhotra
  Self-Help/Motivational, ISBN: 9788180320231
- Meditations by Marcus Aurelius
  Philosophy, ISBN: 9789388118736
- My Experiments with Truth by Mahatma Gandhi
  Biographies & Memoirs, ISBN: 9789387669291
- My Inventions: The Autobiography of Nikola Tesla
  Biographies & Memoirs, ISBN: 9789388118132

Search the book by its ISBN

BESTSELLING NON-FICTION

- Relativity by Albert Einstein
  Science/Physics, ISBN: 9789380914220
- Reminiscences of a Stock Operator by Edwin Lefevre
  Business/Stock Market, ISBN: 9788194764816
- Success Through a Positive Mental Attitude by Napoleon Hill
  Self-Help, ISBN: 9789390492435
- The Art of War by Sun Tzu
  Self-Help, ISBN: 9789380914893
- The Autobiography of a Yogi by Paramahansa Yogananda
  Biographies & Memoirs, ISBN: 9789380914602
- The Diary of a Young Girl by Anne Frank
  Biographies & Memoirs, ISBN: 9789380914312
- The Elements of Style by William Strunk
  Non-Fiction, ISBN: 9789389157123
- The Law of Success by Napoleon Hill
  Self-Help, ISBN: 9788180320927
- The Power of Your Subconscious Mind by Joseph Murphy
  Self-Help, ISBN: 9788180320958
- The Richest Man in Babylon by George S. Clason
  Business & Economics, ISBN: 9789387669369
- The Science of Getting Rich by Wallace D. Wattles
  Self-Help, ISBN: 9788180320972
- The World as I See It by Albert Einstein
  Non-Fiction, ISBN: 9789388118125

Search the book by its ISBN

The Law and the Promise

NEVILLE GODDARD

GENERAL PRESS

Published by

GENERAL PRESS

4805/24, Fourth Floor, Krishna House
Ansari Road, Daryaganj, New Delhi - 110002
Ph : 011-23282971, 45795759
E-mail : generalpressindia@gmail.com

www.generalpress.in

First Edition : 2023

ISBN : 9789354994586

Published by Azeem Ahmad Khan for General Press

Contents

CHAPTER 1

The Law: Imagining Creates Reality

"Man is all Imagination. God is Man and exists in us and we in Him... The Eternal Body of Man is the Imagination, that is, God, Himself."

–Blake

The purpose of the first portion of this book is to show, through actual true stories, how imagining creates reality. Science progresses by way of hypotheses tentatively tested and afterwards accepted or rejected according to the facts of experience. The claim that imagining creates reality needs no more consideration than is allowed by science. It proves itself in performance.

The world in which we live is a world of imagination. In fact, life itself is an activity of imagining; "For Blake", wrote Professor Morrison of the University of St. Andrews, "the world originates in a divine activity identical with what we know ourselves as the activity of imagination", his task being "to open the immortal eyes of man inward into the worlds of thought, into eternity, ever expanding in the bosom of God, the Human Imagination."

Nothing appears or continues in being by a power of its own. Events happen because comparatively stable imaginal activities created them, and they continue in being only as long as they receive such support. "The secret of imagining", writes Douglas Fawcett, "is the greatest of all problems to the solution of which the mystic aspires. Supreme power, supreme wisdom, supreme delight lie in the far-off solution of this mystery."

When man solves the mystery of imagining, he will have discovered the secret of causation, and that is: Imagining creates reality. Therefore, the man who is aware of what he is imagining knows what he is creating; realizes more and more that the drama of life is imaginal – not physical. All activity is at bottom imaginal. An awakened Imagination works with a purpose. It creates and conserves the desirable, and transforms or destroys the undesirable.

Divine imagining and human imagining are not two powers at all, rather one. The valid distinction which exists between the seeming two lies not in the substance with which they operate but in the degree of intensity of the operant power itself. Acting at high tension, an imaginal act is an immediate objective fact. Keyed low, an imaginal act is realized in a time process. But whether imagination is keyed high or low, it is the "ultimate, essentially non-objective Reality from which objects are poured forth like sudden fancies" (Hermann Keyserling, Count, "*The Travel Diary of a Philosopher*"). No object is independent of imagining on some level or levels. Everything in the world owes its character to imagination on one of its various levels.

"Objective reality", writes Fichte, "is solely produced through imagination". Objects seem so independent of our perception of them that we incline to forget that they owe their origin to imagination. The world in which we live is a world of imagination, and man – through his imaginal activities – creates the realities and the circumstances of life; this he does either knowingly or unknowingly.

Men pay too little attention to this priceless gift – The Human Imagination – and a gift is practically nonexistent unless there is a conscious possession of it and a readiness to use it.

All men possess the power to create reality, but this power sleeps as though dead, when not consciously exercised. Men live in the very heart of creation – The Human Imagination – yet are no wiser for what takes place therein.

The future will not be fundamentally different from the imaginal activities of man; therefore, the individual who can summon at will whatever imaginal activity he pleases and to whom the visions of his imagination are as real as the forms of nature, is master of his fate. The future is the imaginal activity of man in its creative march. Imagining is the creative power not only of the poet, the artist, the actor and orator, but of the scientist, the inventor, the merchant and the artisan. Its abuse in unrestrained unlovely image-making is obvious; but its abuse in undue repression breeds a sterility which robs man of actual wealth of experience. Imagining novel solutions to ever more complex problems is far more noble than to run from problems. Life is the continual solution of a continuously synthetic problem.

Imagining creates events. The world, created out of men's imagining, comprises un-numbered warring beliefs; therefore, there can never be a perfectly stable or static state. Today's events are bound to disturb yesterday's established order. Imaginative men and women invariably unsettle a pre-existing peace of mind.

Do not bow before the dictate of facts and accept life on the basis of the world without. Assert the supremacy of your Imaginal acts over facts and put all things in subjection to them. Hold fast to your ideal in your imagination. Nothing can take it from you but your failure to persist in imagining the ideal realized. Imagine only such states that are of value or promise well.

To attempt to change circumstances before you change your imaginal activity, is to struggle against the very nature of things. There can be no outer change until there is first an imaginal change. Everything you do, unaccompanied by an imaginal change, is but futile readjustment of surfaces. Imagining the wish fulfilled brings about a union with that state, and during that union you behave in keeping with your imaginal change. This shows you that an imaginal change will result in a change of behavior. However, your ordinary imaginal alterations as you pass from one state to another are not transformations because each of them is so rapidly succeeded by another in the reverse direction. But whenever one state grows so stable as to become your constant mood, your habitual attitude, then that habitual state defines your character and is a true transformation.

How do you do it? Self-abandonment! That is the secret. You must abandon yourself mentally to your wish fulfilled in your love for that state, and in so doing, live in the new state and no more in the old state. You can't commit yourself to what you do not love, so the secret of self-commission is faith – plus love. Faith is believing what is unbelievable. Commit yourself to the feeling of the wish fulfilled, in faith that this act of self-commission will become a reality. And it must become a reality because imagining *creates* reality.

Imagination is both conservative and transformative. It is conservative when it builds its world from images supplied by memory and the evidence of the senses. It is creatively transformative when it imagines things as they ought to be, building its world out of the generous dreams of fancy. In the procession of images, the ones that take precedence – naturally – are those of the senses. Nevertheless, a present sense impression is only an image. It does not differ in nature from a memory image or the image of a wish. What makes a present sense impression so objectively real is the individual's imagination functioning in it and thinking from it; whereas, in a memory image or a wish, the individual's imagination is not functioning in it and thinking from it, but is functioning out of it and thinking of it.

If you would enter into the image in your imagination, then would you know what it is to be creatively transformative: then would you realize your wish; and then you would be happy. Every image can be embodied. But unless you, yourself, enter the image and think from it, it is incapable of birth. Therefore, it is the height of folly to expect the wish to be realized by the mere passage of time. That which requires imaginative occupancy to produce its effect, obviously cannot be effected without such occupancy. You cannot be in one image and not suffer the consequences of not being in another.

Imagination is spiritual sensation. Enter the image of the wish fulfilled, then give it sensory vividness and tones of reality by mentally acting as you would act were it a physical fact. Now, this is what I mean by spiritual sensation. Imagine that you are holding a rose in your hand. Smell it. Do you detect the odor of roses? Well, if the rose is not there, why is its fragrance in the air?

Through spiritual sensation – that is – through imaginal sight, sound, scent, taste and touch, you can give to the image sensory vividness. If you do this, all things will conspire to aid your harvesting and upon reflection you will see how subtle were the threads that led to your goal. You could never have devised the means which your imaginal activity employed to fulfill itself.

If you long to escape from your present sense fixation, to transform your present life into a dream of what might well be, you need but imagine that you are already what you want to be and to feel the way you would expect to feel under such circumstances. Like the make-believe of a child who is remaking the world after its own heart, create your world out of pure dreams of fancy. Mentally enter into your dream; mentally do what you would actually do, were it physically true. You will discover that dreams are realized not by the rich, but by the imaginative. Nothing stands between you and the fulfillment of your dreams but facts – and facts are the creations of imagining. If you change your imagining, you will change the facts.

Man and his past are one continuous structure. This structure contains all of the facts which have been conserved and still operate below the threshold of his surface mind. For him it is merely history. For him it seems unalterable – a dead and firmly fixed past. But for itself, it is living – it is part of the living age. He cannot leave behind him the mistakes of the past, for nothing disappears. Everything that has been is still in existence. The past still exists, and it gives – and still gives – its results. Man must go back in memory, seek for and destroy the causes of evil, however far back they lie. This going into the past and replaying a scene of the past in imagination as it ought to have been played the first time, I call revision – and revision results in repeal.

Changing your life means changing the past. The causes of any present evil are the unrevised scenes of the past. The past and the present form the whole structure of man; they are carrying all of its contents with it. Any alteration of content will result in an alteration in the present and future.

Live nobly – so that mind can store a past well worthy of recall. Should you fail to do so, remember, the first act of correction or cure is always – "revise." If the past is recreated into the present, so will the revised past be recreated into the present, or else the claim... though your sins are like scarlet, they shall be as white as snow (*Isaiah 1:18*)... is a lie. And it is no lie.

The purpose of the story-to-story Commentary that follows is to link up as briefly as possible the distinct but never disconnected themes of the fourteen chapters into which I have divided the first part of this book. It will serve, I hope, as a thread of coherent thought that binds the whole into proof of its claim! Imagining Creates Reality.

To make such a claim is easily done. To prove it in the experience of others is far sterner. To stir you to use the "Law" constructively in your own life – that is the aim of this book.

CHAPTER 2

Dwell Therein

"My God, I heard this day, that none doth build a stately habitation, but he that means to dwell therein. What house more stately hath there been, or can be, than is Man, to whose creation all things are in decay?"

–George Herbert

I wish it were true of man's noble dreams, but unfortunately – perpetual construction, deferred occupancy – is the common fault of man. Why "build a stately habitation", unless you intend to "dwell therein"? Why build a dream house and not "dwell therein"?

This is the secret of those who lie in bed awake while they dream things true. They know how to live in their dream until, in fact, they do just that. Man, through the medium of a controlled, waking dream, can predetermine his future. That imaginal activity, of living in the feeling of the wish fulfilled, leads man across a bridge of incident to the fulfillment of the dream. If we live in the dream – thinking from it, and not of it – then the creative power of imagining will answer our adventurous fancy, and the wish fulfilled will break in upon us and take us unawares.

Man is all imagination; therefore, man must be where he is in imagination, for his imagination is himself. To realize that imagination is not something tied to the senses or enclosed within the spatial boundary of the body is most important. Although man moves about in space by movement of his physical body, he need not be so restricted. He can move by a change in what he is aware of. However real the scene on which sight rests, man can gaze on one never before witnessed. He can always remove the mountain if it upsets his concept of what life ought to be. This ability to mentally move from things as they are to things as they ought to be, is one of the most important discoveries that man can make. It reveals man as a center of imagining with powers of intervention which enable him to alter the course of observed events, moving from success to success through a series of mental transformations of nature, of others, and himself.

For many years a doctor and his wife "dreamed" about their "stately habitation", but not until they imaginatively lived in it, did they manifest it. Here is their story:

"Some fifteen years ago, Mrs. M. and I purchased a lot on which we built a two-story building housing our office and living area. We left ample space on the lot for an apartment building – if and when our finances would permit. All those years we were busy paying off our mortgage, and at the end of that time had no money for the additional building we still desired so much. It was true that we had an ample savings account which meant security for our business, but to use any part of it for a new building would be to jeopardize that security.

"But now your teaching awakened a new concept, boldly telling us we could have what we most desired through the controlled use of our imagination and that realizing a desire was made more convincing 'without money'. We decided to put it to a test to forget about 'money' and concentrate our attention on the thing we desired most in this world – the new apartment building.

"With this principle in mind, we mentally constructed the new building as we wanted it, actually drawing physical plans so we could better formulate our mental picture of the completed structure. Never forgetting to think from the end (in our case, the completed, occupied building), we took many imaginative trips through our apartment house, renting the units to imaginary tenants, examining in detail every room and enjoying the feeling of pride as friends offered congratulations on the unique planning. We brought into our imaginal scene one friend in particular (*I shall call her Mrs. X*), a lady we had not seen for some time as she had 'given us up' socially, believing us a bit peculiar in our new way of thinking. In our imaginal scene, we took her through the building and asked how she liked it. Hearing her voice distinctly, we had her reply, 'Doctor, I think it is beautiful'.

"One day, while talking together of our building, my wife mentioned a contractor who had constructed several apartment houses in our neighborhood. We knew of him only by the name that appeared on signs adjacent to buildings under construction. But realizing that if we were living in the end, we would not be looking for a contractor, we promptly forgot this angle. Continuing these periods of daily imagining for several weeks, we both felt we were now 'fused' with our desire and had successfully been living in the end.

"One day a stranger entered our office and identified himself as the contractor whose name my wife had mentioned weeks before. In an apologetic manner, he said, 'I don't know why I stopped here. I normally don't go to see people, but rather, people come to see me'. He explained that he passed our office often and had wondered why there wasn't an apartment building on the corner lot. We assured him we would like very much to have such a building there but that we had no money to put into the project, not even the few hundred dollars it would take for plans.

"Our negative response did not faze him and seemingly compelled, he began to figure and devise ways and means to carry out the job, unasked and unencouraged by us. Forgetting the incident, we were quite startled when a few days later this man called, informing us that plans were completed and that the proposed building would cost us thirty thousand dollars! We thanked him politely and did absolutely nothing. We knew we had been 'living imaginatively in the end' of a completed building and that Imagination would assemble that building perfectly without any 'outside' assistance from us. So, we were not surprised when the contractor called again the next day to say he had found a set of blueprints in his files that fitted our needs perfectly with few alterations. This, we were informed, would save us the architect's fee for new plans. We thanked him again and still did nothing.

"Logical thinkers would insist that such negative response from prospective customers would completely end the matter. Instead, two days later, the contractor again called with the news that he had located a finance company willing to cover the necessary loan with the exception of a few thousand dollars. It sounds incredible, but we still did nothing. For – remember – to us this building was completed and rented, and in our imagination we had not put one penny into its construction.

"The balance of this tale reads like a sequel to 'Alice In Wonderland', for the contractor came to our office the next day and said, as though presenting us with a gift, 'You people are going to have that new building anyway. I've decided to finance the balance of the loan myself. If this is agreeable, I'll have my lawyer draw up the papers, and you can pay me back out of net profits from rentals'.

"This time we did do something! We signed the papers, and construction began immediately. Most of the apartment units were rented before final completion, and all but one occupied the day of completion. We were so thrilled by the seemingly miraculous events of the past few months that for a while we didn't understand this seeming 'flaw' in our imaginal picture. But knowing what we had already accomplished through the power of imagining, we immediately conceived another imaginal scene and in it, this time, instead of showing the party through the unit and hearing the words 'we'll take it', we ourselves in imagination visited tenants who had already moved in that apartment. We allowed them to show us through the rooms and heard their pleased and satisfied comments. Three days later that apartment was rented.

"Our original imaginary drama had objectified itself in every detail save one, and that one became a reality when, one month later, our friend, Mrs. X, surprised us with a long overdue visit, expressing her desire to see our new building. Gladly we took her through, and at the end of the tour heard her speak the line we had heard in our imagination so many weeks before, as with emphasis on each word, she said, 'Doctor, I think it is beautiful'.

"Our dream of fifteen years was realized. And we know, now, that it could have been realized any time within those fifteen years if we had known the secret of imagining and how to 'live in the end' of desire. But now it was realized – our one big desire was objectified. And we did not put one penny of our own money into it." – Dr. M.

Through the medium of a dream – a controlled, waking dream – the Doctor and his wife created reality. They learned how to live in their dream house as, in fact, now they do. Although help seemingly came from without, the course of events was ultimately determined by the imaginal activity of the Doctor and his wife. The participants were drawn into their imaginal drama because it was dramatically necessary that they should be. Their imaginal structure demanded it.

"All things by a law divine In one another's being mingle." (*–Percy Bysshe Shelley, "Love's Philosophy"*)

The following story illustrates the way in which a lady prepared her "stately habitation" by imaginatively sleeping in it – or "dwelling therein".

"A few months ago, my husband decided to place our home on the market. The main object for the move which we had discussed many times was to find a home large enough for the two of us, my mother and my aunt, in addition to ten cats, three dogs and one parakeet. Believe it or not, the contemplated move was my husband's idea as he loved my mother and aunt and said I was at their house most of the time anyway, so 'why not live together and pay one tax bill?' I liked the idea tremendously, but I knew that this new home would have to be something very special in size, location and arrangement, as I insisted on privacy for all concerned.

"So at the moment I was undecided whether to sell our present home or not, but I didn't argue, as I knew quite well from past experience with imagining that our house would never sell until I stopped 'sleeping' in it. Two months and four or five real-estate brokers later, my husband had 'given up' on the sale of our house and so had the brokers. At this point, I had convinced myself I now wanted the change, so for four nights, in my imagination, I went to sleep in the kind of home I would like to own. On the fifth day, my husband had an appointment at a friend's home and while there, met a stranger who 'just happened' to be looking for a house in the hills. He was, of course, brought swiftly back to see our house which he walked through once and said, 'I'll buy it'. This didn't make us very popular with the brokers, but that was all right with me, as I was happy to keep the broker's commission in the family! We moved within ten days and stayed with my mother while looking for our new home.

"We listed our requirements with every agent on the Sunset Strip only (*because I wouldn't move out of the area*) and each one of them without exception informed us we were both mad. It was entirely impossible, they said, to find an older home of English style with two separate living rooms, separate apartments, a library, and built on a flat knoll with enough ground space to fence for large dogs – and located in one particular area. When we told them the price we would pay for this house they just looked sad.

"I said that wasn't all we wanted. We wanted wood paneling all through the house, a huge fireplace, a magnificent view and seclusion – no close neighbors, please. At this point the lady agent would giggle and remind me that there was no such house, but if there were, they would realize five times what we were willing to pay. But I knew there was such a house – because my imagination had been sleeping in it, and if I am my imagination, then I had been sleeping in it.

"By the second week we had exhausted five real estate offices, and the gentleman in the sixth office was looking a little wild when one of his partners who had not spoken until then said, 'Why don't you show them the place up King's Road?' A third partner in the office laughed sourly and said, 'That property isn't even listed. And besides – the old lady would throw you off the property. She's got two acres up there and you know she wouldn't split.'

"Well, I didn't know what she wouldn't split, but my interest had been aroused by the street name for I liked that particular area best of all. So I asked why not just take a look anyway, for laughs. As we drove up the street and turned off onto a private road, we approached a large two-story house built of redwood and brick, English in appearance, surrounded by tall trees and sitting alone and aloof on its own knoll, viewing the city below from all of its many windows. I felt a peculiar excitement as we walked to the front door and were greeted by a lovely woman who graciously asked us in.

"I do not think I breathed for the next minute or two, for I had walked into the most exquisite room I had ever seen. The solid redwood walls and the brick of a great fireplace rose to a height of twenty-eight feet terminating in an arched ceiling joined together by huge redwood beams. The room was straight out of Dickens, and I could almost hear Christmas carolers singing on the balcony of the upstairs dining room which looked out over the living room. A great cathedral window gave a view of sky, mountains and city far below, and the beautiful old redwood walls glowed in the sunlight. We were shown through a spacious apartment on the lower floor with connecting library, separate entrance and separate patio. Two staircases led upward to a long hall opening into two separated bedrooms and baths, and at the end of the hall was – yes – a second living room, opening out onto a second patio screened by trees and redwood fencing.

"Built on two acres of beautifully landscaped grounds, I began to understand what the agent had meant by saying, 'she wouldn't split' for on one acre stood a large swimming pool and pool house completely separated from the main house but undoubtedly belonging to it. It did, indeed, seem to be an impossible situation as we did not want two acres of highly taxable property plus a swimming pool a block away from the house.

"Before we left, I walked through that magnificent living room, once more going up the stairs to the dining room balcony. I turned, and looking down saw my husband standing by the fireplace, pipe in hand, with an expression of perfect satisfaction on his face. I placed my hands on the balcony railing and watched him for a moment.

"When we were back in the real estate office, the three agents were ready to close for the day, but my husband detained them saying, 'Let's make her an offer anyway. Maybe she will split the property. What can we lose?' One agent left the office without a word. Another said, 'The idea is ridiculous'. The agent we had originally talked to said, 'Forget it. It's a pipe dream'. My husband is not easily annoyed but when he is, there is no more stubborn creature on earth. He was now annoyed. He sat down, slammed his hand on a desk and roared, 'It's your business to submit offers, isn't it?' They agreed that this was so and finally promised to submit our offer on the property.

"We left, and that night – in my imagination – I stood on that dining room balcony and looked down at my husband standing by the fireplace. He looked up at me and said, 'Well, honey, how do you like our new home?' I said, 'I love it'. I continued to see that beautiful room and my husband in it and 'felt' the balcony railing gripped in my hands until I fell asleep.

"The next day, as we were having dinner in my mother's house, the telephone rang and the agent, in an unbelieving voice, informed me that we had just purchased a house. The owner had split the property right down the middle, giving us the house and the acre it stood on for the price we offered."... J.R.B."

> ...dreamers often lie in bed awake, while they do dream things true." (*approx., William Shakespeare, "Romeo and Juliet"*)

One must adopt either the way of imagination or the way of sense. No compromise or neutrality is possible. "He who is not for me is against me" (*Matthew 12:30, Luke 11:23*). When man finally identifies himself with his Imagination rather than his senses, he has at long last discovered the core of reality.

I have often been warned by self-styled "realists" that man will never realize his dream by simply imagining that it is already here. Yet, man can realize his dream by simply imagining that it is already here. That is exactly what this collection of stories proves; if only men were prepared to live imaginatively in the feeling of the wish fulfilled, advancing confidently in their controlled waking-dream, then the power of imagining would answer their adventurous fancy and the wish fulfilled would break in upon them and take them unawares.

Nothing is more continuously wonderful than the things that happen every day to the man with imagination sufficiently awake to realize their wonder. Observe your imaginal activities. Imagine better than the best you know, and create a better world for yourself and others. Live as though the wish had come, even though it is yet to come, and you will shorten the period of waiting. The world is imaginal, not mechanistic. Imaginal acts – not blind fate – determine the course of history.

CHAPTER 3

Turn the Wheel Backward

"Oh, let your strong imagination turn the great wheel backward, until Troy unburn."

–Sir John Collings Squire, "*The Birds*"

"All life is, throughout the ages, nothing but the continuing solution of a continuous synthetic problem."

–H.G. Wells

The perfectly stable or static state is always unattainable. The end attained objectively always realizes more than the end the individual originally had in view. This, in turn, creates a new situation of inner conflict, needing novel solutions to force man along the path of creative evolution. "His touch is infinite and lends a yonder to all ends." (*George Meredith, "Hymn to Colour"*) Today's events are bound to disturb yesterday's established order. The creatively active imagination invariably unsettles a pre-existing peace of mind.

The question may arise as to how, by representing others to ourselves as better than they really were, or mentally rewriting a letter to make it conform to our wish, or by revising the scene of an accident, the interview with the employer, and so on – could change what seems to be the unalterable facts of the past, but remember my claims for imagining: Imagining Creates Reality. What it makes, it can unmake. It is not only conservative, building a life from images supplied by memory – it is also creatively transformative, altering a theme already in being.

The parable of the unjust steward (Luke 16:1-8) gives the answer to this question. We can alter our world by means of a certain "illegal" imaginal practice, by means of a mental falsification of the facts – that is, by means of a certain intentional imaginal alteration of that which we have experienced. All this is done in one's own imagination. This is a form of falsehood which not only is not condemned, but is actually approved in the gospel teaching. By means of such a falsehood, a man destroys the causes of evil and acquires friends and on the strength of this revision proves, judging by the high praise the unjust steward received from his master, that he is deserving of confidence.

Because imagining creates reality, we can carry revision to the extreme and revise a scene that would be otherwise unforgivable. We learn to distinguish between man – who is all imagination – and those states into which he may enter. An unjust steward, looking at another's distress, will represent the other to himself as he ought to be seen. Were he, himself, in need – he would enter his dream in his imagination and imagine what he would see and how things would seem and how people would act – 'after these things should be'. Then, in this state he would fall asleep, feeling the way he would expect to feel, under such circumstances.

Would that all the Lord's people were unjust stewards – mentally falsifying the facts of life to deliver individuals forevermore. For the imaginal change goes forward, until at length the altered pattern is realized on the heights of attainment. Our future is our imaginal activity in its creative march. Imagine better than the best you know.

To revise the past is to re-construct it with new content. Man should daily relive the day as he wished he had lived it, revising the scenes to make them conform to his ideals. For instance, suppose today's mail brought disappointing news. Revise the letter. Mentally rewrite it and make it conform to the news you wish you had received. Then, in imagination, read the revised letter over and over again and this will arouse the feeling of naturalness; and imaginal acts become facts as soon as we feel natural in the act. This is the essence of revision and revision results in repeal. This is exactly what F.B. did:

"Late in July I wrote to a real estate agent of my desire to sell a piece of land which had been a financial burden to me. His negative reply listed all the reasons why sales were at a standstill in that area, and he forecast a bleak period of waiting until after the first of the year.

"I received his letter on a Tuesday, and – in my imagination – I rewrote it with words indicating that the agent was eager to take my listing. I read this revised letter over and over, and I extended my imaginal drama using your theme of the Four Mighty Ones of our Imagination – from your book 'Seedtime and Harvest' – the Producer, the Author, the Director and the Actor.

"In my imaginal scene as Producer, I suggested the theme, 'The lot is sold for a profit. As the Author, I wrote this simple scene which, to me, implied fulfillment: Standing in the real estate office,

I extended my hand to the agent and said, 'Thank you, sir', and he replied, 'It was a pleasure doing business with you'. As Director, I rehearsed myself as Actor until that scene was vividly real and I felt the relief which would be mine if the burden were really lifted.

"Three days later, the agent I had originally written phoned me saying he had a deposit for my lot at the price I had specified. I signed the papers in his office the next day, extended my hand and said, 'Thank you, sir'. The agent replied, 'It was a pleasure doing business with you'.

"Five days after I had constructed and enacted an imaginal scene, it became a physical reality and was played word for word just as I had heard it in my imagination. The feeling of relief and joy came – not so much from selling the property – but from the incontrovertible proof that my imagined drama worked."... F.B.

If the thing accomplished were all, how futile! But F.B. discovered a power within himself that can consciously create circumstances.

By mentally falsifying the facts of life, man moves from passive reaction to active creation; this breaks the wheel of recurrence and builds a cumulatively enlarging future. If man does not always create in the full sense of the word, it is because he is not faithful to his vision, or else he thinks of what he wants rather than from his wish fulfilled.

Man is such an extraordinary synthesis, partly tied by his senses, and partly free to dream that his internal conflicts are perennial. The state of conflict in the individual is expressed in society.

Life is a romantic adventure. To live creatively, imagining novel solutions to ever more complex problems is far nobler than to restrain or kill out desire. All that is desired can be imagined into existence.

"Wouldst thou be in a Dream, and yet not sleep?" (John Bunyan, *"The Pilgrim's Progress"*). Try to revise your day every night before falling asleep. Try to visualize clearly and enter into the revised scene which would be the imaginal solution of your problem. The revised imaginal structure may have a great influence on others, but that is not your concern. The "other" influenced in the following story is profoundly grateful for that influence. L.S.E. writes:

"Last August, while on a 'blind date' I met the man I wanted to marry. This happens sometimes, and it happened to me. He was everything I had ever thought of as desirable in a husband. Two days after this enchanted evening, it was necessary for me to change my place of residence because of my work, and that same week the mutual friend who had introduced me to this man, moved away from the city. I realized that the man I had met probably did not know of my new address, and frankly, I was not sure he knew my name.

"After your last lecture, I spoke to you of this situation. Although I had plenty of other 'dates' I could not forget this one man. Your lecture was based on revising our day; and after speaking to you, I determined to revise my day, every day. Before going to sleep that night, I felt I was in a different bed, in my own home, as a married woman – and not as a single working girl, sharing an apartment with three other girls. I twisted an imaginary wedding band on my imaginary left hand, saying over and over to myself, 'This is wonderful! I really am Mrs. J.E.!' and I fell asleep in what was – a moment before – a waking dream.

"I repeated this imaginary scene for one month, night after night. The first week in October he 'found' me. On our second date, I knew my dreams were rightly placed. Your teaching tells us to live in the end of our desire until that desire becomes 'fact' so although I did not know how he felt toward me, I continued, night after night, living in the feeling of my dream realized.

"The results? In November he proposed. In January we announced our engagement; and the following May we were married. The loveliest part of it all, however, is that I am happier than I ever dreamed possible; and I know in my heart, he is too."... Mrs. J.E.

By using her imagination radically, instead of conservatively – by building her world out of pure dreams of fancy – , rather than using images supplied by memory, she brought about the fulfillment of her dream. Common sense would have used images supplied by her memory, and thereby perpetuated the fact of lack in her life. Imagination created what she desired out of a dream of fancy. Everyone must live wholly on the level of imagination, and it must be consciously and deliberately undertaken.

> "... Lovers and madmen have such seething brains, Such shaping fantasies, that apprehend more than cool reason over comprehends." (William Shakespeare, *"A Midsummer Night's Dream"*)

If our time of revision be well spent, we need not worry about results – our fondest hopes will be realized.

"Art thou real, Earth? Am I? In whose dream do we exist?..." (approx., Frank Kendon, *"The Time Piece"*)

There is no inevitable permanence in anything. Both past and present continue to exist only because they are sustained by

"Imagining" on some level or other; and a radical transformation of life is always possible by man revising the undesirable part of it.

In his letter, Mr. R.S. questions this subject of influence:

"During your current series of lectures, trouble developed with collections on one of my Trust Deeds. The security, a house and lot, was neglected and run down. The owners were apparently spending their money in bars while their two little girls, aged nine and eleven, were noticeably uncared for. However, forgetting appearances, I began to revise the situation. In my imagination I drove my wife past the property and said to her, 'Isn't the yard beautiful? It's so neat and well cared for. Those people really show their love for their home. This is one Trust Deed we will never have to worry about'. I would 'see' the house and lot as I wanted to see it – a place so lovely, it gave me a warm glow of pleasure. Every time the thought of this property came to me, I repeated my imaginal scene.

"After I had been practicing this revision for some time, the woman who lived in the house had an automobile accident; while she was in the hospital her husband disappeared. The children were cared for by neighbors; and I was tempted to visit the mother in the hospital to reassure her of assistance, if necessary. But how could I, when my imaginary scene implied that she and her family were happy, successful and obviously contented? So I did nothing but my daily revision. A short while after leaving the hospital, the woman and her two daughters disappeared also. Payments were sent in on the property and a few months later she reappeared with a wedding certificate and a new husband. At this writing, all payments are right up to date. The two little girls are obviously happy and well cared for, and a room has been added to the property by the owners giving our Trust Deed additional security.

"It was mighty nice to solve my problem without threats, unkind words, eviction, or worry about the little girls; but was there something in my imagining that sent that woman to the hospital?"... R.S.

Any imaginal activity acquiring intensity through our concentrated attention to clarity of the end desired tends to overflow into regions beyond where we are; but we must leave it to take care of such imaginal activity itself. It is marvelously resourceful in adapting and adjusting means to realize itself. Once we think in terms of influence rather than of clarity of the end desired, the effort of imagination becomes an effort of will and the great art of imagining is perverted into tyranny.

The buried past usually lies deeper than our surface mind can plumb. But fortunately, for this lady, she remembered and proved that the "made" past can also be "unmade" through revision.

"For thirty-nine years I had suffered from a weak back. The pain would increase and decrease but would never leave completely. The condition had progressed to the point where I used medical treatment almost constantly; the doctor would put the hip right for the moment but the pain simply would not go away. One night I heard you speak of revision and wondered to myself if a condition of almost forty years could be revised. I had remembered that at the age of three or four years I had fallen backward from a very high swing and had been quite ill at that time because of a serious hip injury. From that time on I had never been completely free from pain and had paid many a dollar to alleviate the condition, to no avail.

"This year, during the month of August, the pain had become more intense and one night I decided to test myself and attempt to revise that 'ancient' accident which had been the cause of so much distress in pain and costly medical fees most of my adult life. Many nights passed before I could 'feel' myself back to the age of childhood play. But I succeeded. One night I actually 'felt' myself on that swing feeling the rush of wind as the swing rose higher and higher. As the swing slowed down, I jumped forward landing solidly and easily on my feet. In the imaginal action I ran to my mother and insisted that she come watch what I could do. I did it again, jumping down from the swing and landing safely on my two feet. I repeated this imaginal act over and over until I fell asleep in the doing of it.

"Within two days the pain in my back and hip began to recede and within two months pain no longer existed for me. A condition that had plagued me for more than thirty-nine years, that had cost a small fortune in attempted cure – was no more."... L.H.

It is to the pruning shears of revision that we owe our prime fruit. Man and his past are one continuous structure. This structure contains all of the past which has been conserved and still operates below the threshold of his senses to influence the present and the future of his life. The whole is carrying all of its contents with it; any alteration of content will result in an alteration in the present and the future. The first act of correction or cure is always "Revise." If the past can be recreated into the present, so can the revised past. And thus the Revised Past appears within the very heart of her present life; not Fate but a revised past brought her good fortune.

Make results and accomplishment the crucial test of true imagination and your confidence in the power of imagination to create reality will grow gradually from your experiments with revision confronted by experience. Only by this process of experiment can you realize the potential power of your awakened and controlled imagination.

"How much do you owe my master?" He said, "A hundred measures of oil". And he said to him, "Take your bill, and sit down quickly and write fifty!" (*Luke 16:5, 6*). This parable of the unjust steward urges us to mentally falsify the facts of life, to alter a theme already in being. By means of such imaginative falsehoods, a man "acquires friends" (*Luke 16:9*). As each day falls, mentally revise the facts of life and make them conform to events well worthy of recall; tomorrow will take up the altered pattern and go forward until at length it is realized on the heights of attainment.

The reader will find it worthwhile to follow these clues – imaginal construction of scenes implying the wish fulfilled, and imaginative participation in these scenes until tones of reality are reached. We are dealing with the secret of imagining, in which man is seen awakening into a world completely subject to his imaginative power.

Man can understand recurrence of events well enough (*the building of a world from images supplied by memory*) – things remaining as they are. This gives him a sense of security in the stability of things. However, the presence within him of a power which awakens and becomes what it wills, radically changing its form, its environment and the circumstances of life, inspires in him a feeling of insecurity, a dreadful fear of the future.

Now, "it is high time to awake out of sleep" (*Romans 13:11*) and put an end to all the unlovely creations of sleeping Man. Revise each day. "Let your strong imagination turn the great wheel backward until Troy unburn." (–(Sir) John Collings Squire, "*The Birds*")

CHAPTER 4

There is no Fiction

"The distinction between what is real and what is imaginary is not one that can be finally maintained... all existing things are, in an intelligible sense, imaginary."

–John S. Mackenzie

There is no fiction. If an imaginal activity can produce a physical effect, our physical world must be essentially imaginal. To prove this would require merely that we observe our imaginal activities and watch to see whether or not they produce corresponding external effects. If they do, then we must conclude that there is no fiction. Today's imaginal drama – fiction – becomes tomorrow's fact.

If we had this wider view of causation – that causation is mental, not physical – that our mental states are causative of physical effects, then we would realize our responsibility as a creator and imagine only the best imaginable.

Fable enacted as a sort of stage-play in the mind is what causes the physical facts of life. Man believes that reality resides in the solid objects he sees around him, that it is in this world that the drama of life originates, that events spring suddenly into existence, created moment by moment out of antecedent physical facts. But causation does not lie in the external world of facts. The drama of life originates in the imagination of man. The real act of becoming takes place within man's imagination and not without.

The following stories could define "causation" as the assemblage of mental states, which occurring, creates that which the assemblage implies.

The foreword from Walter Lord's "*A Night to Remember*" illustrates my claim, "*Imagining Creates Reality.*"

"In 1898, a struggling author, named Morgan Robertson, concocted a novel about a fabulous Atlantic liner, far larger than any that had ever been built. Robertson loaded his ship with rich and complacent people and then wrecked it one cold April night on an iceberg. This somehow showed the futility of everything, and in fact, the book was called 'FUTILITY' when it appeared that year, published by the firm of M. F. Mansfield.

"Fourteen years later, a British shipping company, named the White Star Line, built a steamer remarkably like the one in Robertson's novel. The new liner was 66,000 tons displacement; Robertson's was 70,000 tons.

"The real ship was 882.5 feet long; the fictional one was 800 feet. Both could carry about 3,000 people, and both had enough lifeboats for only a fraction of this number. But, then this didn't seem to matter because both were labeled 'unshakable!'

"On April 19, 1912, the real ship left Southampton on her maiden voyage to New York. Her cargo included a priceless copy of the Rubaiyat of Omar Khayyam and a list of passengers collectively worth $250 million dollars. On her way over, she, too, struck an iceberg and went down on a cold April night.

"Robertson called his ship the Titan; the White Star Line called its ship the Titanic."

Had Morgan Robertson known that Imagining Creates Reality, that today's fiction is tomorrow's fact, would he have written the novel Futility? "In the moment of the tragic catastrophe", writes Schopenhauer, "the conviction becomes more distinct to us than ever that life is a bad dream from which we have to awake." And the bad dream is caused by the imaginal activity of sleeping humanity.

Imaginal activities may be remote from their manifestation and unobserved events are only appearance. Causation as seen in this tragedy is elsewhere in space-time. Far off from the scene of action, invisible to all, was Robertson's imaginal activity, like a scientist in a control-room directing his guided missile through Space-Time.

Who paints a picture, writes a play or book
Which others read while he's asleep in bed
O' the other side of the world – when they o'erlook
His page the sleeper might as well be dead;
What knows he of his distant unfelt life?
What knows he of the thoughts his thoughts are raising,
The life his life is giving, or the strife
Concerning him – some cavilling, some praising?
Yet which is most alive, he who's asleep
Or his quick spirit in some other place,
Or score of other places, that doth keep
Attention fixed and sleep from others chase?

Which is the "he" – the "he" that sleeps, or "he"
That his own "he" can neither feel nor see?
–Samuel Butler

Imaginative writers communicate not their vision of the world but their attitudes which result in their vision. Just a short while before Katherine Mansfield died, she said to her friend Orage:

"There are in life as many aspects as attitudes toward it; and aspects change with attitudes... Could we change our attitude, we should not only see life differently, but life itself would come to be different. Life would undergo a change of appearance because we ourselves had undergone a change in attitude... Perception of a new pattern is what I call a creative attitude towards life."

"Prophets", wrote Blake, "in the modern sense of the word, have never existed. Jonah was no prophet in the modern sense, for his prophesy of Nineveh failed. Every honest man is a prophet; he utters his opinion both of private & public matters. Thus: If you go on So, the result is So. He never says, such a thing shall happen let you do what you will. A Prophet is a Seer, not an Arbitrary Dictator." The function of the Prophet is not to tell us what is inevitable, but to tell us what can be built up out of persistent imaginal activities.

The future is determined by the imaginal activities of humanity, activities in their creative march, activities which can be seen in "Your dreams and the visions of your head as you lay in bed" (*Daniel 2:28*). "Would that all the Lord's people were prophets" (*Numbers 11:29*) in the true sense of the word like this dancer who now, from the summit of his realized ideal, sights yet higher peaks that are to be scaled. After you have read this story you will understand why he is so confident that he can predetermine any materialistic future he desires and why he is equally sure that others give reality to what were otherwise a mere figment of his imagination, that there exists and can exist nothing outside imagining on some level or other. Nothing continues in being save what imagining supports. "… The mind can make Substance, and people planets of its own with beings brighter than have been, and give a breath to forms which can outlive all flesh…" (*Lord G. Byron*)

As my story begins at the age of nineteen I was a mildly successful dancing teacher and continued in this static state for almost five years. At the end of this time I met a young lady who talked me into attending your lectures. My thought, upon hearing you say 'Imagining creates reality', was that the entire idea was ridiculous. However, I decided to accept your challenge and disprove your thesis. I bought your book 'Out of This World' and read it many times. Still unconvinced, I set myself a rather ambitious goal. My present position was as an instructor with the Arthur Murray Dance Studio and my goal was to own a franchise and be boss of an Arthur Murray studio myself!

"This seemed the most unlikely thing in the world as franchises were extremely difficult to secure, but on top of this fact, I was completely without the necessary funds to begin such an operation. Nevertheless. I assumed the feeling of my wish fulfilled as night after night, in my imagination, I went to sleep managing my own studio. Three weeks later a friend called me from Reno, Nevada. He had the Murray Studio there and said it was too much for him to cope with alone. He offered me a partnership and I was delighted; so delighted, in fact, that I hastened to Reno on borrowed money and promptly forgot all about you and your story of Imagination!

"My partner and I worked hard and were very successful, but after a year I was still not satisfied, I wanted more. I began thinking of ways and means to get another studio. All my efforts failed. One night as I retired, I was restless and decided to read. As I looked through my collection of books I noticed your slender volume, 'Out of This World'. I thought of the 'silly nonsense' I had gone through one year ago before getting my own studio. GETTING MY OWN STUDIO! The words in my mind electrified me! I reread the book that night and later, in my imagination, I heard my superior praise the good job we had done in Reno and suggest we acquire a second studio as he had a second location ready for us if we desired to expand. I re-enacted this imaginal scene nightly without fail. Three weeks from the first night of my imaginal drama, it materialized – almost word for word. My partner accepted the new studio in Bakersfield and I had the Reno Studio alone. Now I was convinced of the truth of your teaching and never again will I forget.

"Now I wanted to share this wonderful knowledge – of imaginal power with my staff. I tried to tell them of the marvels they could accomplish, but I was unable to reach many although one fantastic incident resulted from my efforts to tell this story. A young teacher told me he believed my story but said it would have probably happened anyway in time. He insisted the entire theory was nonsense but stated that if I could tell him something of an incredible nature that would actually happen and which he could witness – then he would believe. I accepted his challenge and conceived a truly fantastic test.

"The Reno Studio is the most insignificant in the entire Murray system because of the small population count in the city itself. There are over three hundred Murray Studios in the country with much larger populations, therefore providing greater possibilities to draw from. So, my test was this. I told the teacher that within the next three months, at the time of a national dance convention, the little Reno Studio would be the foremost topic of conversation at that convention. He calmly stated this was quite impossible.

"That night when I retired, I felt myself standing before a tremendous audience. I was speaking on 'Creative Imagining' and felt the nervousness of being before such a vast audience; but I also felt the wonderful sensation of audience acceptance. I heard the roar of applause and as I left the stage, I saw Mr. Murray, himself come forward and shake my hand. I re-enacted this entire drama night after night. It began to take on the 'tones of reality' and I knew I had done it again!

"My imaginal drama materialized down to the last detail.

"My little Reno Studio was the 'talk' of the convention and I did appear on that stage just as I had done in my imagination. But even after this unbelievable but actual happening, the young teacher who threw me the challenge remained unconvinced. He said it had all happened too naturally! And he was sure it would have happened anyway!

"I did not mind his attitude because his challenge had given me another opportunity to prove, at least to myself, that Imagining does Create Reality. From that time on, I continued with my ambition to own the 'largest Arthur Murray Dance Studio in the world'! Night after night, in my imagination, I heard myself accepting a studio franchise for a great city. Within three weeks Mr. Murray called me and offered a studio in a city of one and a half million people! It is now my goal to make my studio the greatest and biggest in the entire system. And, of course, 'I know it will be done – through my Imagination'!"... E.O.L., Jr.

"Imagining", writes Douglas Fawcett, "may be hard to grasp, being 'quicksilver-like' it vanishes into each of its metamorphoses and thereby displays its transformative magic." We must look beyond the physical fact for the imagining which has caused it. For one year E.O.L., Jr. lost himself in his metamorphosis but fortunately he remembered "the silly nonsense" he had gone through before getting his own studio... and re-read the book.

Imaginal acts on the human level need a certain interval of time to develop but imaginal acts, whether committed to print or locked in the bosom of a hermit, will realize themselves in time.

Test yourself, if only out of curiosity. You will discover the "Prophet" is your own imagining and you will know "there is no fiction".

"We should never be certain that it was not some woman treading in the wine-press who began that subtle change in men's mind... or that the passion, because of which so many countries were given to the sword, did not begin in the mind of some shepherd boy, lighting up his eyes for a moment before it ran upon its way." – William Butler Yeats

There is no fiction. Imagining fulfills itself in what our lives become.

"And now I have told you before it takes place, so that when it does take place, you may believe." (*John 14:29*)

The Greeks were right: "The Gods have come down to us in the likeness of men!" (*Acts 14:11*). But they have fallen asleep and do not realize they might they wield by their imaginal activities.

> "Real are the dreams of Gods, and smoothly pass
> Their pleasure in a long immortal dream."
>
> –John Keats

E.B., an author, is fully aware that "today's fiction can become tomorrow's fact". In this letter, she writes:

"One Spring, I completed a novelette, sold it and forgot it. Not until many long months later did I sit down and nervously compare some 'facts' in my fiction with some 'facts' in my life! Please read a brief outline of my created story. Then compare it with my personal experience.

"The heroine of my story took a vacation trip to Vermont. To the small city of Stowe, Vermont, to be exact. When she reached her destination she was faced with such unpleasant behavior on the part of her companion that she either had to continue her lifetime pattern of allowing another's selfish demand dominate her or to break that pattern and leave. She broke it and returned to New York. When she returned (and the story continues) events took shape in a proposal of marriage which she happily accepted.

"For my part of this tale... as small events evolved... I began to remember the dictates of my own pen and in significant relationship. This is what happened to me! I received an invitation from a friend offering me a vacation at her summer place in Vermont. I accepted and was not startled, at first, when I learned her 'summer place' was in the city of Stowe. When I arrived, I found my hostess in such a highly nervous state I realized I was faced with either a wretched summer or the choice of 'walking out' on her. Never before in my life had I been strong enough to ignore what I thought were the claims of duty and friendship – but this time I did and without ceremony returned to New York. A few days after I returned to my home, I, too, received a proposal of marriage. But at this point fact and fiction parted. I refused the offer! I know, Neville, there is no such thing as fiction."... E.B.

"Forgetful is green earth, the gods alone remember everlastingly... by their great memories the gods are known." (George Meredith, "*Ballads and Poems of Tragic Life*")

Ends run true to their imaginal origins – we reap the fruit of forgotten blossom-time. In life the events do not come up always where we have strewn the seed; so that we may not recognize our own harvest. Events are the emergence of a hidden imaginal activity. Man is free to imagine whatever he desires. This is why, despite all fatalists and misguided prophets of doom, all awakened men know that they are free. They know that they are creating reality. Is there a scriptural passage to support this claim? Yes:

"And it came to pass, as he interpreted to us, so it was." (*Genesis 41:13*)

W. B. Yeats must have discovered that "there is no fiction", for after describing some of his experiences in the conscious use of imagination, he writes: "If all who have described events like this have not dreamed, we should rewrite our histories for all men, certainly all imaginative men, must be forever casting forth enchantments, glamours, illusions; and all men, especially tranquil men, who have no powerful egotistic life must be continually passing under their power. Our most elaborate thoughts, elaborate purposes, precise emotions, are often as I think, not really ours, but have on a sudden come up, as it were, out of hell or down out of heaven..." ("*Ideas of Good and Evil*")"

There is no fiction." Imagine better than the best you know.

CHAPTER 5

Subtle Threads

"...all you behold; tho' it appears without, it is Within; In your Imagination, of which this World of Mortality is but a Shadow."

–Blake

Nothing appears or continues in being by a power of its own. Events happen because comparatively stable imaginal activities created them, and they continue in being by virtue of the support they receive from such imaginal activities. The part which imagining the wish fulfilled plays in consciously creating circumstances is obvious in this series of stories.

You will see how the telling of one story of the successful use of imagination can serve as a spur and a challenge to others to "try" it and "see".

One night a gentleman rose in my audience. He said that he had no question to ask but would like to tell me something. This was his story:

When he came out of the Armed Forces after World War II he got a job that gave him take-home pay of $25.00 a week.

After ten years he was making $600.00 a month. At that time he bought my book "Awakened Imagination" and read the chapter "The Pruning Shears of Revision."

Through the daily practice of "Revision", as set forth there, he was able to tell my audience two years later that his income was equal to that of the President of the United States.

In my audience sat a man who, by his confession, was broke. He had read the same book, but he suddenly realized he had done nothing with the use of his imagination to solve his financial problem.

He decided he would try to imagine himself as the winner of the 5-10 pool at Caliente Race Track. In his words: "In this pool, one attempts to pick winners in the fifth through the tenth races. So this is what I did: In my imagination I stood, sorting my tickets and feeling as I did so, that I had each of the six winners. I enacted this scene over and over in my imagination, until I actually felt 'goose pimples'. Then I 'saw' the cashier giving me a large sum of money which I placed beneath my imaginary shirt. This was my entire imaginal drama; and for three weeks, night after night, I enacted this scene and fell asleep in the action.

"After three weeks I traveled physically to the Caliente Race Track, and on that day every detail of my imaginative play was actually realized. The only change in the scene was that the cashier gave me a check for a total of $84,000.00 instead of currency."... T.K.

After my lecture the night this story was told, a man in the audience asked me if I thought it possible for him to duplicate T.K.'s experience. I told him he must decide the circumstances of his imaginal scene himself but that whatever scene he chose, he must create a drama he could make natural to himself and imagine the end intently with all the feeling he could muster; he must not labor for the means to the end but live imaginatively in the feeling of the wish fulfilled.

One month later he showed me a check for $16,000.00 which he had won in another 5-10 pool at the same Caliente Race Track the previous day.

This man had a sequel to his most interesting duplication of T.K.'s good fortune. His first win took care of his immediate financial difficulties although he wanted more money for future family security. Also, and more important to him, he wanted to prove that this had not been an "accident". He reasoned that if his good luck could happen a second time in succession, the so-called "law of percentages" would give way to proof for him that his imaginal structures were actually producing this miraculous "reality". And so he dared to put his imagination to a second test. He continues:

"I wanted a sizeable bank account and this, to me, meant 'seeing' a large balance on my bank statements. Therefore, in my imagination I enacted a scene which took me into two banks. In each bank I would 'see' an appreciative smile meant for me from the bank manager as I walked into his establishment and I would 'hear' the teller's cordial greeting. I would ask to see my statement. In one bank I 'saw' a balance of $10,000.00. In the other bank I 'saw' a balance of $15,000.00.

"My imaginal scene did not end there. Immediately after seeing my bank balances I would turn my attention to my horse racing system which, through a progression of ten steps, would bring my winnings to $11,533.00 with a starting capital of $200.00.

"I would divide the winnings into twelve piles on my desk. Counting the money in my imaginary hands I would put

$1,000.00 in each of eleven piles and the remaining five-hundred thirty-three dollars in the last pile. My 'imaginative accounting' would amount to $36,533.00 including my bank balances.

"I enacted this entire imaginative scene each morning, afternoon and night for less than one month, and, on March second, I went to the Caliente track again. I made out my tickets, but strangely enough and not knowing why I did so, I duplicated six more tickets exactly like the six already made out but in the tenth selection I made a 'mistake' and copied two tickets twice. As the winners came in, I held two of them – each paying $16,423.50. I also had six consolation tickets, each paying $656.80. The combined total amounted to $36,788.00. My imaginary accounting one month before had totaled $36,533.00. Two points of interest, most profound to me, were that by seeming accident I had marked two winning tickets identically and also, that at the end of the ninth race (which was one of the major winners) the trainer attempted to 'scratch' the horse, but the Stewards denied the trainer's request."... A.J.F.

How subtle were the threads that led to his goal? Results must testify to our imagining or we really are not imagining the end at all. A.J.F. faithfully imagined the end, and all things conspired to aid his harvesting. His "mistake" in copying a winning ticket twice, and the Steward's refusal to allow the trainer's request were events created by the imaginal drama to move the plan of things forward to its goal.

"Chance", wrote Belfort Bax, "may be defined as that element in the reality change – that is, in the flowing synthesis of events – which is irreducible to law or the causal category."

To live wisely we must be aware of our imaginal activities or, at any rate, of the end which they are tending. We must see to it that it is the end we desire.

Wise imagining identifies itself only with such activities that are of value or promise well. However much man seems to be dealing with a material world, he is actually living in a world of imagination. When he discovers that it is not the physical world of facts but imaginal activities which shape his life, then the physical world will no longer be the reality, and the world of imagination no longer the dream.

> *"Does the road wind uphill all the way?*
> *Yes, to the very end.*
> *Will the day's journey take the whole long day?*
> *From morn to night, my friend."*
>
> –Christina Georgina Rossetti, "*Uphill*"

CHAPTER 6

Visionary Fancy

"The Nature of Visionary Fancy, or Imagination, is very little known, & the External nature & permanence of its ever Existent Images is consider'd as less permanent than the things of Vegetative & Generative Nature; yet the Oak dies as well as the Lettuce, but Its Eternal image & Individuality never dies, but renews by its seed; just so the Imaginative Image returns by the seed of Contemplative Thought."

–Blake

The images of our imagination are the realities of which any physical manifestation is only the shadow. If we are faithful to vision, the image will create for itself the only physical manifestation of itself it has a right to make. We speak of the "reality" of a thing when we mean its material substance. That is exactly what an imaginist means by its "unreality" or shadow.

Imagining is spiritual sensation. Enter into the feeling of your wish fulfilled. Through spiritual sensation – through your use of imaginal sight, sound, scent, taste and touch – you will give to your image the sensory vividness necessary to produce that image in your outer or shadow world.

Here is the story of one who was faithful to his vision. F.B. being a true imaginist, remembered what he had heard in his imagination. Thus he writes:

"A friend who knows my passionate fondness for opera tried to get Kirsten Flagstad's complete recording of Tristan and Isolde for me at Christmas. In over a dozen record stores he was told the same thing: 'RCA Victor is not reissuing this recording and there have been no copies available since June. On December 27th, I determined to prove your principle again by getting the album I desired so intensely. Lying down in my living room, I mentally walked into a record shop I patronize and asked the one salesman whose face and voice I could recall, 'Do you have Flagstad's complete Isolde?' He replied, 'Yes, I have.' "That ended the scene and I repeated it until it was 'real' to me.

"Late that afternoon, I went to that record shop to physically enact the scene. Not one detail supplied by the senses had encouraged me to believe I could walk out of that shop with those records. I had been told last September by the same salesman in the same shop the same story my friend had received there before Christmas. Approaching the salesman I had seen in imagination that morning, I said, 'Do you have Flagstad's complete Isolde?' He replied, 'No, we haven't.' Without saying anything audible to him, I said inwardly, 'That's not what I heard you say!'

"As I turned to leave the shop, I noticed on a top shelf what I thought to be an advertisement of this set of records and remarked to the salesman, 'If you don't have the merchandise, you shouldn't advertise it.' 'That's right', he replied, and as he reached up to take it down, discovered it to be a complete album, with all five records! The scene wasn't played exactly as I had constructed it, but the result confirmed what my imagined scene implied. How can I thank you?"... F.B.

After reading F.B.'s letter, we must agree with Anthony Eden that "An assumption, though false, if persisted in, will harden into fact." F.B.'s fancy, fusing with the sense-field of the record shop, enriched aspects of it and made them 'his' – what he perceived.

Our future is our imagining in its creative march. F.B. used his imagination for a conscious purpose representing life as he desired it to be and thereby affecting life instead of merely reflecting it. So sure was he that his imaginal drama was the reality – and the physical act but a shadow – that when the salesman said "No, we haven't", F.B. mentally said, "That's not what I heard you say!" He not only remembered what he had heard, but he was still remembering it. Imagining the wish fulfilled is the seeking that finds, the asking that receives, the knocking to which is opened. He saw and heard what he desired to see and hear; and would not take "No, we haven't" for an answer.

The imaginist dreams while awake. He is not the servant of his Vision, but the master of the direction of his attention. Imaginative constancy controls perception of events in space-time. Unfortunately, most men are...

> *"Ever changing, like a joyless eye*
> *That finds no object worth its constancy..."*
> –Percy Bysshe Shelley, "*To The Moon*"

Mrs. G.R., too, had imaginatively heard what she wanted to physically hear and knew the outer world must confirm it. This is her story:

"Some time ago we advertised our home for sale which was necessary for us to buy a larger property on which we had placed a deposit. Several people would have bought our home immediately but we were obliged to explain that we could not close any deal until we learned whether or not our offer for the property we wanted had been accepted. At this time, a broker called and literally begged us to allow him to show our home to a client of his who was eager for this location and would be glad to pay even more than we were asking. We explained our situation to the broker and to his client; they both stated they did not mind waiting for our deal to be consummated. "The broker asked us to sign a paper which he said was not binding in any way but would give him first chance at the sale if our other deal went through. We signed the paper and later learned that in California Real Estate law nothing could have been more binding. A few days later our deal for the new property fell through so we notified this broker and his verbal response was, 'Well, just forget it'. Two weeks later he filed suit against us for fifteen hundred dollars commission. Trial date was set and we asked for a jury trial.

"Our attorney assured us he would do all he could, but that the law on this particular point was so stringent that he could not see any possibility of our winning the case. "When time for the trial arrived, my husband was in the hospital and could not appear with me in our defense. I had no witnesses; but the broker brought three attorneys and a number of witnesses into court against us. Our attorney now told me we had not the slightest chance to win.

"I turned to my imagination, and this is what I did. Completely disregarding all that had been said by attorneys, witnesses and the judge who seemed to favor the plaintiff, I thought only of the words I wanted to hear. In my imagination, I listened intently and heard the foreman of the jury say, 'We find the defendant not guilty'. I listened until I knew it was true. I closed my mind's ear to everything said in that courtroom and heard only those words, 'We find the defendant not guilty!' The jury deliberated from noon recess until four-thirty that afternoon, and all during those hours I sat in the courtroom and heard those words over and over in my imagination. When the jurors returned, the Judge asked the foreman to stand and give their verdict. The foreman stood up and said, 'We find the defendant NOT guilty'."... Mrs. G.R.

> *"If there were dreams to sell*
> *What would you buy?"*
> –Thomas Lovell Beddoes, "*Dream-Pedlary*"

Would you not buy your wish fulfilled? Your dreams are without price and without money. By locking up the jury in her imagination – hearing only what she wanted to hear, she called the jury to unanimity on her behalf. Imagining being the reality of all that exists, with it the lady achieved her wish fulfilled.

Hebbel's statement that "the poet creates from contemplation" is true of imaginists as well. They know how to utilize their video-audio hallucinations to create reality.

Nothing is so fatal as conformity. We must not allow ourselves to be girt about by the ringed fixity of fact. Change the image, and thereby change the fact. R.O. employed the art of seeing and feeling to create her vision in imagination.

"A year ago I took my children to Europe leaving my furnished apartment in the care of my maid. When we returned a few months later to the United States, I found my maid and all my furniture gone. The apartment superintendent stated that the maid had had my furniture moved 'by my request'. There was nothing I could do at the moment, so I took my children and moved into a hotel. I, of course, reported the incident to the police and, also, brought in private detectives on the case. Both organizations investigated every moving company and every storage warehouse in New York City, but to no avail. There seemed to be absolutely no trace of my furniture, nor of my maid.

"Having exhausted all outside sources, I remembered your teaching and decided I would try using my imagination in this matter. So, while seated in my hotel room, I closed my eyes and imagined myself in my own apartment, sitting in my favorite chair and surrounded by all of my personal furnishings. I looked across the living room at the piano on which I kept pictures of my children. I would continue to stare at my piano until the entire room became vividly real to me. I could see my children's pictures and actually feel the upholstery of the chair in which, in my imagination, I sat.

"The next day, as I came out of my bank, I turned to walk in the direction of my vacant apartment instead of toward my hotel. When I reached the corner, I discovered my 'mistake' and was just about to turn back when my attention was drawn to a very familiar pair of ankles. Yes, the ankles belonged to my maid. I walked up to her and took hold of her arm. She was quite frightened, but I assured her all I wanted from her was my furniture. I called a taxi and she took me to the place in which her friends had stored my furnishings. In one day, my imagination had found what an entire big city police force and private investigators could not find in weeks."... R.O.

This lady knew of the secret of imagining before she called in the police, but imagining – in spite of its importance – was forgotten owing to attention being fixed on facts. However, what reason failed to find by force, imagining found without effort.

Nothing merely goes on – including the sense of loss – without its imaginal support. By imagining that she was seated in her own chair, in her own living room, surrounded by all of her own furnishings, she withdrew the imaginal support she had given to her sense of loss; and by this imaginal change she recovered her lost furniture and re-established her home.

Your imagination is most creative when you imagine things as you desire them to be, building a new experience out of a dream of fancy. To build such a dream of fancy in her imagination, F.G. brought to play all of her senses – sight, sound, touch, smell – even taste. This is her story:

"Since childhood, I have dreamed of visiting far-away places. The West Indies, particularly, fired my fancy, and I would revel in the feeling of actually being there. Dreams are wonderfully inexpensive and as an adult I continued to dream my dreams, for I had no money or time to make them 'come true'. Last year I was taken to the hospital in need of surgery. I had heard your teaching and, while recuperating, had decided to intensify my favorite daydream while I had time on my hands. I actually wrote to the Alcoa Steamship Line asking for free travel folders and pored over them, hour after hour, choosing the ship and the stateroom and the seven ports I desired most to see. I would close my eyes and, in my imagination, would walk up the gangplank of that ship and feel the movement of water as the great liner pushed its way into free ocean. I heard the thud of waves breaking against the sides of the ship, felt the steaming warmth of a tropical sun on my face and smelled and tasted salt in the air as we all sailed through blue waters.

"For one solid week, confined to a hospital bed, I lived the free and happy experience of actually being on that ship. Then, the day before my release from the hospital, I tucked the colored folders away and forgot them. Two months later, I received a telegram from an advertising agency telling me I had won a contest. I remembered having deposited a contest coupon some months before in a neighborhood supermarket but had completely forgotten the act. I had won first prize and – wonder of wonders – it entitled me to a Caribbean cruise sponsored by the Alcoa Steamship Line. But the wonder didn't stop there. The very stateroom I had imaginatively lived in and moved about in while confined to a hospital bed had been assigned to me. And to make an unbelievable story even more unbelievable, I sailed on the one ship I had chosen – which stopped in not one, but all of the seven ports I had desired to visit!"... F.G.

"To travel is the privilege, not of the rich but of the imaginative." (Stephen Berrien Stanton, "*The Essential Life*", 1908)

CHAPTER 7

Moods

"This is an age in which the mood decides the fortunes of people rather than the fortunes decide the mood."

–Sir Winston Churchill

Men regard their moods far too much as effects and not sufficiently as causes. Moods are imaginal activities without which no creation is possible. We say that we are happy because we have achieved our goal; we do not realize that the process works equally well in the reverse direction – that we shall achieve our goal because we have assumed the happy feeling of the wish fulfilled.

Moods are not only the result of the conditions of our life; they are also the causes of those conditions. In "The Psychology of Emotions", Professor Ribot writes, "An idea which is only an idea produces nothing and does nothing; it only acts if it is felt, if it is accompanied by an effective state, if it awakens tendencies, that is to say, motor elements."

The lady in the following story so successfully felt the feeling of her wish fulfilled, she made her mood the character of the night – frozen in a delightful dream.

"Most of us read and love fairy stories, but we all know that stories of improbable riches and good fortune are for the delight of the very young. But arc they? I want to tell you of something unbelievably wonderful that happened to me through the power of my imagination – and I am not 'young' in years. We live in an age which believes in neither fable nor magic, and yet everything I could possibly want in my wildest day-dreams was given to me by the simple use of what you teach – that 'imagining creates reality' and that 'feeling' is the secret of imagining.

"At the time this wonderful thing happened to me I was out of a job and had no family to fall back upon for support. I needed just about everything. To find a decent job I needed a car to look for it, and though I had a car, it was so worn out it was ready to fall apart. I was behind in my rent; I had no proper clothes to seek a job; and today it's no fun for a woman of fifty-five to apply for a job of any kind. My bank account was almost depleted and there was no friend to whom I could turn.

"But I had been attending your lectures for almost a year and my desperation forced me to put my imagination to the test. Indeed, I had nothing to lose. It was natural for me, I suppose, to begin by imagining myself having everything I needed. But I needed so many things and in such short order that I found myself exhausted when I finally got through the list, and by that time I was so nervous I could not sleep. One lecture night I heard you tell of an artist who captured the 'feeling', or 'word', as you called it, of 'isn't it wonderful!' in his personal experience. "I began to apply this idea to my case. Instead of thinking of and imagining every article I needed, I tried to capture the 'feeling' that something wonderful was happening to me – not tomorrow, not next week – but right now.

I would say over and over to myself as I fell asleep, 'Isn't it wonderful! Something marvelous is happening to me now!' And as I fell asleep I would feel the way I would expect to feel under such circumstances.

"I repeated that imaginary action and feeling for two months, night after night, and one day in early October I met a casual friend I hadn't seen for months who informed me he was about to leave on a trip to New York. I had lived in New York many years ago and we talked of the city a few moments and then parted. I completely forgot the incident. One month later, to the day, this man called at my apartment and simply handed me a Certified Check in my name for twenty-five hundred dollars. After I got over the initial shock of seeing my name on a check for so much money, the story that unfolded seemed to me like a dream. It concerned a friend I had not seen nor heard from in more than twenty-five years. This friend of my past, I now learned, had become extremely wealthy in those twenty-five years. Our mutual acquaintance who had brought the check to me had met him quite by accident during the trip to New York last month. During their conversation they spoke of me, and for reasons I was not to know (for to this day I have not heard from him personally and have never attempted to contact him) this old friend decided to share a portion of his great wealth with me.

"For the next two years, from the office of his attorney, I received monthly checks so generous in amount they not only covered every necessary requirement of daily living, but left much over for all the lovely things of life: a car, clothes, a spacious apartment – and best of all, no need to earn my daily bread.

"This past month I received a letter and some legal papers to be signed which provide the continuation of this monthly income for the rest of my natural life!"... T.K.

"If the fool would persist in his folly He would become wise." –*William Blake*

Sir Winston calls on us to act on the assumption that we already possess that which we sought, to "assume a virtue", if we have it not (*William Shakespeare's 'Hamlet'*). Is this not the secret of "miracles"? Thus the man with palsy was told to rise, to take up his bed and walk – to mentally act as if he were healed (*Matthew 9:1-8; Mark 2:1-13; Luke 5:18-25; John 5:1-17*); and when the actions of his imagination corresponded with the actions which he would physically perform were he healed – he was healed.

"This is a story about which some may say, 'it would have happened anyway', but those who read it carefully will find room to wonder. It begins one year ago as I left Los Angeles to visit my daughter in San Francisco. Instead of the happy-natured individual she had always been, I found her in deep distress. Not knowing the cause of her anguish and not wishing to ask, I waited until she told me that she was in great financial trouble and must have three thousand dollars immediately. I am not a poor woman but I didn't have much cash I could put my hands on that quickly. Knowing my daughter, I knew she would not have accepted it anyway. I offered to borrow the money for her, but she refused and instead asked me to help her in 'my way'... she meant using my imagination, for I had often told her of your teaching and some of my words must have struck home.

"I immediately agreed on this plan with the provision that she would help me help her. We decided on an imaginal scene we could both practice that involved 'seeing' money coming to her from everywhere. We felt money was flooding toward her from every corner, until she was in the middle of a 'sea' of money, but we did this always with the feeling of 'Joy' for anyone concerned and we had no thought of means, only happiness for all.

"The idea seemed to catch fire with her, and I know she was responsible for what happened a few days later. She was certainly transformed back to the happy, confident mood that was natural to her, though there was no evidence of any real money coming in at the time. I left to return home in the East.

"When I arrived home I called my mother (a lovely young lady of ninety-one) who immediately asked me to come and see her. I wanted a day's rest but she couldn't wait; it had to be now. Of course I went, and after greeting me, she handed me a check for three thousand dollars made out to my daughter! Before I could speak, she handed me three additional checks totaling fifteen hundred dollars made in favor of my daughter's children. Her reason? She explained that she had suddenly decided the day before to give what she had in cash to those she loved while she was still 'here' to know of their happiness in receiving it!

"It would have happened anyway? No – not like this. Not within days of my daughter's frantic need, and then her sudden transformation to a mood of joy.

I know that her imaginal act caused this wonderful change – bringing not only great joy to the receiver but to the giver as well."

"P.S... I almost forgot to add that among the checks so lavishly given, was one for me too, for three thousand dollars!"... M.B.

The boundless opportunities opened by recognizing the shift of the focus of imagining are beyond measure. There are no boundaries. The drama of life is an imaginal activity in which we bring to pass by our moods rather than by our physical acts. Moods so ably guide all towards that which they affirm, they may be said to create the circumstances of life and dictate the events. The mood of the wish fulfilled is the high tide which lifts us easily off the bar of the senses where we usually lie stranded. If we are aware of the mood and know this secret of imagining, we may announce that all that our mood affirms will come to pass.

The following story is by a mother who succeeded in sustaining a seemingly "playful" mood with startling results.

"Surely you've heard the 'old wives' tale about warts: That, if a wart is bought, it will disappear? I've known this story from childhood but not until I heard your lectures did I realize the truth hidden in the old tale. My boy, a lad of ten, had many large ugly warts on his legs causing an irritation which had plagued him for years. I decided that my sudden 'insight' could be used to his advantage. A boy has a lot of faith in his mother as a rule so I asked him if he would like to be rid of his warts. He quickly said, 'Yes', but he did not want to go to a doctor. I asked him to play a little game with me, that I would pay him a sum of money for each wart. This suited him fine; he said – 'he didn't see how he could lose!' We arrived at a fair price, he thought, and then I said, 'Now, I'm paying you good money for those warts; they no longer belong to you. You never keep property belonging to someone else so you can no longer keep those warts. They will disappear. It may take a day, two days or a month; but remember that I've bought them and they belong to me.'

"My son was delighted with our game and the results sound like something read in old musty books on magic. But, believe me, within ten days the warts began to fade, and, at the end of one month every wart on his body had completely disappeared!

"There is a sequel to this story for I've bought warts from many people. They, too, thought it great fun and accepted my five, seven or ten cents a wart. In each case the wart disappeared – but really – only one person believes me when I tell him his Imagination, alone, took away the warts. That one person is my young son."... J.R.

Man imagining himself into a mood takes on himself the results of the mood. If he does not imagine himself into the mood, he is ever free of the result. The great Irish mystic, A.E. (*George William Russell*), wrote in "The Candle of Vision": "I became aware of a swift echo or response to my own moods in circumstance which had seemed hitherto immutable in its indifference... I could prophesy from the uprising of new moods in myself that I, without search, would soon meet people of a certain character, and so I met them. Even inanimate things were under the sway of these affinities." But man need not wait for the uprising of new moods in himself; he can create happy moods at will.

CHAPTER 8

Through the Looking Glass

"A man that looks on glass,
On it may stay his eye;
Or if he pleaseth, through it pass,
And then the heav'n espy."

–George Herbert "*The Elixir*"

Objects, to be perceived, must first penetrate in some manner our brain; but we are not – because of this – interlocked with our environment. Although normal consciousness is focused on the senses and is usually restricted to them, it is possible for man to pass through his sense fixation into any imaginal structure which he conceives and so fully occupies it that it is more alive and more responsive than that on which his senses "stay his eye". If this were not true, man would be an automaton reflecting life, never affecting it. Man, who is all Imagination, is not tenant to the brain, but landlord; he need not rest content with the appearance of things; he can go beyond perceptual to conceptual awareness.

This ability, to pass through the mechanical reflective structure of the senses, is the most important discovery man can make. It reveals man as a center of imagining with powers of intervention which enable him to alter the course of observed events moving from success to success through a series of mental transformations in himself. Attention, the spearhead of imagining, may be either attracted from without as his senses "stay his eye" or directed from within "if he pleases" and through the senses pass into the wish fulfilled.

To move from perceptual awareness, or things as they seem, to conceptual awareness, or things as they ought to be, we imagine as vivid and as life-like a representation as possible of what we would see, hear, and do, were we physically present, and physically experiencing things as they ought to be and imaginatively participate in that scene. The following story tells of one who went "through the glass" and broke the chains that bound her.

"Two years ago I was taken to the hospital with a serious blood clot condition which apparently had affected the entire vascular system causing hardening of arteries and arthritis. A nerve in my head was damaged and my thyroid enlarged. Doctors could not agree on the cause of this condition, and all their treatments were completely ineffective. I was forced to give up my every enjoyable activity and remain in bed most of the time. My body, from hips to toes, felt as though it was encased and bound by tight wires, and I couldn't put my feet on the floor without wearing heavy hip-length elastic stockings.

"I knew something of your teaching and tried very hard to apply what I had heard, but as my condition grew worse and I could no longer attend any of your lectures, my despondency grew deeper. One day a friend sent me a postcard picturing the scene of a lovely beach by the ocean. The picture was so beautiful,

I looked and looked at it and began to remember past summer days at the seashore with my parents. For a moment, the post-card picture seemed to become animated and flooding memories of myself running free on the beach filled my mind. I felt the impact of my bare feet against the hard wet sand; I felt the icy water running over my toes and heard the crash of waves breaking on shore. This imaginal activity was so satisfying to me as I lay in bed that I continued to imagine this wonderful scene, day after day, for about one week.

"One morning, I moved from my bed to a couch and had started to sit up when I was seized with such an excruciating pain my entire body became paralyzed.

I could neither sit up nor lie down. This terrible pain lasted for more than a full minute, but when it stopped – I was free! It seemed as if all the wires binding my legs had been cut. One moment I was bound; the next moment I was free. Not by degrees, but instantly."... V.H.

"We walk by faith, not by sight." –2 Cor. 5:7

When we walk by sight, we know our way by objects which our eyes see. When we walk by faith, we order our life by scenes and actions which only imagination sees.

Man perceives by the Eye of Imagination or by Sense. But two mental attitudes to perception are possible, the creative imaginative effort which meets with an imaginative response, or the unimaginative "staying of the eye" which merely reflects.

Man has within him the principle of life and the principle of death. One is the imagination building its imaginal structures out of the generous dreams of fancy. The other is the imagination building its imaginal structures from images reflected by the chill wind of fact. One creates. The other perpetuates. Man must adopt either the way of faith or the way of sight. To the extent that man builds from dreams of fancy, he is alive; and, therefore, the development of the faculty to pass through the reflective glass of the senses is an increase of life.

It follows that restricting the imagination by "staying the eye" on the reflective glass of the senses is a reduction of life.

The specious surface of fact reflects rather than discloses, deflecting the "Eye of Imagination" from the truth that sets man free (*John 8:32*). "The Eye of Imagination", if not deflected, looks on what ought to be there, not what is. However familiar the scene on which sight rests, the "Eye of Imagination" could gaze on one never before witnessed.

It is this "Eye of Imagination" and only this that can free us from the sense fixation of outer things which completely dominates our ordinary existence and keeps us looking on the reflective glass of facts. It is possible to pass from thinking of to thinking from; but the crucial matter is thinking from, i.e., experiencing the state, for that experience means unification; whereas in thinking of there is always subject and object – the thinking individual and the thing thought of.

Self-abandonment. That is the secret. We have to abandon ourselves to the state, in our love for the state, and in so doing live the life of the state and no more our present state. Imagination seizes upon the life of the state and gives itself to the expression of the life of that state.

Faith plus Love is self-commission. We can't commit ourselves to what we do not love. "Never would you have made anything if you had not loved it." ("For you love all the things that are, and despise nothing which you have made: For never would you have made anything, if you hated it.", "*Book of Wisdom*" 11:24).

And to make the state alive, one must become it. "I live, yet not I, God lives in me: and the life I now live in the flesh, I live by the faith of God, Who loved me and gave Himself for me." ("I am crucified with Christ: nevertheless I live; yet not I, but Christ lives in me: and the life which I now live in the flesh I live by the faith of the Son of God, Who loved me, and gave Himself for me.", Galatians 2:20) God loved man, His created, and became man in faith that this act of self-commission would transform the created into the creative.

We must be "imitators of God as dear children" (*Ephesians 5:1*) and commit ourselves to what we love, as God Who loved us committed Himself to us. We must BE the state to experience the state.

The center of conscious imagining can be shifted and what are now mere wishes – imaginal activities keyed low – brought into penetrative focus and entered. Entrance commits us to the state. The possibilities of such shifting of the center of imagining are startling. The activities concerned are psychical throughout. The shifting of the center of imagining is not brought about by spatial travel but by a change in what we are aware of. The boundary of the world of sense is a subjective barrier. So long as the senses take notice, the Eye of Imagination is deflected from the truth. We do not get far unless we let go.

This lady "let go" with immediate and miraculous results.

"Thank you for the 'golden key'. It has released my brother from the hospital, from pain and probable death, for he was facing a fourth major operation with little hope of recovery, I was very concerned and attempting to use what I had learned about my Imagination, I first asked myself what my brother truly desired: 'Does he want to continue in this body or does he desire to be free of it?' The question revolved itself over and over in my mind and suddenly I felt that he would like to continue remodeling his kitchen which he had been contemplating before his confinement in the hospital. I knew my question had been answered, so I began to imagine from that point.

"Attempting to 'see' my brother in the busy activity of remodeling, I suddenly found myself gripping the back of a kitchen chair I had used many times when 'something' happened, then suddenly I found myself standing beside my brother's bed in the hospital. This was the last place I would have wanted to be, physically or mentally, but there I was and my brother's hand reached up and clasped my hand tightly as I heard him say, 'I knew you would come, Jo'.

It was a well hand I clasped, strong and sure, and the joy that filled and spilled over in my voice as I heard myself say, 'It's all better now. You know it'. My brother didn't answer, but I distinctly heard a voice say to me, 'Remember this moment'. I seemed to awake then, back in my own home.

"This took place the night after he had entered the hospital. The following day his wife telephoned me saying, 'It is unbelievable! The doctor can't account for it, Jo, but no operation is necessary. He's so improved that they have agreed to release him tomorrow.' The following Monday, my brother went back to his work and has been perfectly well since that day."... J.S.

Not facts – but dreams of fancy shape our lives.

She needed no compass to find her brother, nor tools to operate, only the "Eye of Imagination". In the world of sense we see what we have to see; in the world of Imagination we see what we want to see; And seeing it, we create it for the world of sense to see. We see the outer world automatically. Seeing what we want to see demands voluntary and conscious imaginative effort. Our future is our own imaginal activity in its creative march. Common sense assures us that we are living in a solid and sensible world but this so seemingly solid world is – in reality – imaginal through and through.

The following story proves that it is possible for an individual to transfer the center of imagining to some greater or lesser degree to a distant area, and not only do so without moving physically, but to be visible to others who are present at that point in space-time. And, if this be a dream, then,

> *"Is all that we see or seem*
> *But a dream within a dream?"*
>
> –Edgar Allan Poe

"Seated in my living room in San Francisco, I imagined I was in my daughter's living room in London, England. I surrounded myself so completely with that room which I knew intimately, that I suddenly found myself actually standing in it. My daughter was standing by her fireplace, her face turned away from me. A moment later she turned and our eyes met. I saw such a startled, frightened expression on her face that I, too, became emotionally upset and immediately found myself back in my own living room in San Francisco.

"Five days later, I received an airmail letter from my daughter which had been written on the day of my experiment with imaginal travel. In her letter she told me she had 'seen' me in her living room that day just as real as though I were actually standing there in the flesh. She confessed she had been very frightened and that before she could speak, I had vanished. The time of this 'visitation', as she gave it in her letter, was exactly the time I had begun the imaginative action allowing, of course, for the difference in time between the two points. She explained that she told her husband of this amazing experience and he insisted that she write to me immediately as he stated, 'Your mother must have died or is dying'. But I wasn't 'dead' or 'dying', but very much alive and very excited by this marvelous experience."... M.L.J.

> *"Nothing can act but where it is:*
> *with all my heart; only where is it?"*
>
> –Thomas Carlyle

Man is All Imagination. Therefore, a man must be where he is in imagination, for his Imagination is himself. Imagination is active at and through any state that it is aware of. If we take shifting of awareness seriously, there are possibilities beyond belief. The senses join man in forced and unholy wedlock to what, were he imaginatively awake, he would put asunder. We need not feed on sense-data. Shift the focus of awareness and see what happens. However little we move mentally, we should perceive the world under a slightly changed aspect. Awareness is usually moved about in space by movement of the physical organism but it need not be so restricted. It can be moved by a change in what we are aware of.

Man is manifesting the power of Imagination whose limits he cannot define. To realize that the Real Self – Imagination – is not something enclosed within the spatial boundary of the body is most important. The foregoing story proves that when we meet a person in the flesh, that his Real Self need not be present in space where his body is. It also shows that sense-perception can be thrown into operation outside of the normal physical means, and that the sense-data produced is of the same kind as those which occur in normal perception. The idea in the mother's mind which started the whole process going was the very definite idea of being in the place where her daughter lived. And if the mother really were in that place, and if the daughter were present, then she would have to be perceptible to her daughter.

We can only hope to understand this experience in imaginal, and not in mechanical or materialistic terms. The mother imagined 'elsewhere' as being 'here'. London was just as 'here' to her daughter living 'there' as San Francisco was 'here' to the mother living 'there'.

It hardly ever crosses our minds that this world might be different in essence from what common sense tells us it so obviously is. Blake writes: "I question not my Corporeal or Vegatative Eye any more than I would Question a Window concerning a Sight. I look thro' it and not with it." This looking through the eye not only shifts consciousness to other parts of "this world" but to "other worlds" as well. Astronomers must wish they knew more of this "looking through the eye", this mental traveling that mystics practice so easily.

> *I travel'd thro' a Land of Men,*
> *A Land of Men & Women too,*
> *And heard & saw such dreadful things*
> *As cold Earth wanderers never knew.*
>
> –William Blake, '*The Mental Traveller*'

Mental traveling has been practiced by awakened men and women since the earliest days. Paul states: "I know a man in Christ who fourteen years ago was caught up to the third heaven – whether in the body or out of the body I do not know, God knows." 2 Cor.12 Paul is telling us that he is that man and that he traveled by the power of imagination or Christ. In his next letter to the Corinthians, he writes: "Test yourselves. Do you not realize that Jesus Christ is in you?" (*2 Corinthians 13:5*). We need not be 'dead' in order to enjoy spiritual privileges. "Man is All Imagination and God is Man." (William Blake, from "*Annotations to Berkeley*"). Test yourselves as this mother did.

Sir Arthur Eddington said that all we have a right to say of the external world is that it is a "shared experience". Things are more or less 'real' according to the extent to which they are capable of being shared with others or with ourselves at another time. But there is no hard and fast line.

Accepting Eddington's definition of reality as "shared experience", the above story is as 'real' as the earth or a color for it was shared by both mother and daughter. The range of imagining is such that I must confess that I do not know what limits, if any, there are to its ability to create reality.

All these stories show us one thing – that an imaginal activity implying the wish fulfilled must start in the imagination apart from the evidence of the senses in that Journey that leads to the realization of desire.

CHAPTER 9

Enter Into

"If the Spectator would Enter into these Images in his Imagination, approaching them on the Fiery Chariot of his Contemplative Thought, if he could... make a Friend & Companion of one of these Images of wonder, which always entreats him to leave mortal things (as he must know) then would he arise from his Grave, then would he meet the Lord in the Air & then he would be happy."

–Blake

Imagination it seems will do nothing that we wish until we enter into the image of the wish fulfilled.

Does not this entering into the image of the wish fulfilled resemble Blake's "Void outside of Existence which if enter'd into Englobes itself & becomes a Womb?" Is this not the true interpretation of the mythical story of Adam and Eve? Man and his emanation? Are not man's dreams of fancy his Emanation, his Eve in whom "He plants himself in all her Nerves, just as a Husbandman his mould; And she becomes his dwelling place and garden fruitful seventy fold?" (William Blake, "*The Mental Traveller*")

The secret of creation is the secret of imagining – first, desiring and then assuming the feeling of the wish fulfilled until the dream of fancy, 'the Void outside existence', is enter'd and 'englobes itself and becomes a womb, a dwelling place and garden fruitful seventy fold'. Note well that Blake urges us to enter into these images. This entering into the image makes it 'englobe itself and become a womb'. Man, by entering a state, impregnates it and causes it to create what the union implies. Blake tells us that these images are 'Shadowy to those who dwell not in them, mere possibilities; but to those who enter into them they seem the only substances...'

On my way to the West Coast, I stopped in Chicago to spend the day with friends. My host was recovering from a severe illness and his doctor advised him to move to a one-story house. Acting upon the doctor's advice, he had purchased a one-story house suited to his needs; but he now was confronted with the fact that there seemed to be no buyer for his large three-story home. When I arrived, he was very discouraged. In trying to explain the law of constructive imagining to my host and his wife, I told them the story of a very prominent New York woman who had come to see me concerning the rental of her apartment. She maintained a lovely city apartment and a country home, but it was absolutely essential that she rent her apartment if she and her family were to spend the summer at their country home. (Neville Goddard, "*The Power of Awareness*", Ch. 23, "Case Histories – 5")

In previous years, the apartment had been rented without any difficulty early in the spring, but at the time she came to see me, the season for summer sublets was seemingly over. Although the apartment had been in the hands of good real estate agents, no one had seemed interested in renting it. I told her what to do in her imagination. She did it and, in less than twenty-four hours, her apartment was rented.

I explained how she, by the constructive use of her imagination, had rented her apartment. At my suggestion, before she went to sleep that night in her apartment in the city, she imagined she was lying in her bed in her country home. In her imagination, she viewed the world from the country house rather than from the city apartment. She smelled the fresh country air. She made this so real that she actually drifted off to sleep feeling that she was in the country. That was on a Thursday night. At nine o'clock the following Saturday morning, she phoned me from her country home and told me that on Friday a highly desirable tenant, who met all of her requirements, not only rented her apartment, but rented it on the one condition that he could move in that very day.

I suggested to my friends that they build an imaginal structure as this woman had done, and that was to sleep, imagining they were physically present in their new home, feeling they had sold their old home. I explained to them the wide difference between thinking of the image of their new house, and thinking from the image of their new house. Thinking of it is a confession they are not in it; thinking from it is proof that they are in it. Entering into the image would give substance to the image. Their physical occupancy of the new house would follow automatically.

I explained that what the world looks like depends entirely on where man is when he makes his observation. And man, being "All Imagination", must be where he is in imagination. This concept of causation disturbed them, for it smacked of magic or superstition, but they promised they would try it. I left that night for California and the following evening the conductor on the train in which I was traveling handed me a telegram. It read: "House sold midnight last". One week later, they wrote and told me that the very night I left Chicago they fell asleep physically in the old house but mentally in the new, viewing the world from the new home, imagining how things would "sound" if this were true. They were awakened that very night from their sleep to be told the house was sold.

Not until the image is entered, until Eve is known, does the event burst upon the world. The wish fulfilled must be conceived in the imagination of man before the event can evolve out of what Blake calls 'the Void'.

This next story proves that by shifting the focus of her imagining, Mrs. M.F. entered physically into where she had persisted in being imaginatively.

"Soon after our marriage, my husband and I decided that our greatest joint desire was a year in Europe. This objective may seem reasonable to a lot of people, but to us – tied to a narrow sphere of limited finances – it seemed not only unreasonable, but completely ridiculous. Europe might as well have been another planet. But I had heard your teaching, so I persisted in falling asleep in England! Why England necessarily, I cannot tell, except that I had seen a current motion picture featuring the area around Buckingham Palace and had promptly fallen in love with the scene. All I did in my imagination was to stand quietly outside the great iron gates and feel the cold metal bars gripped tightly in my hands as I viewed the Palace.

"For many, many nights I felt an intense joy at 'being' there and fell asleep in this happy state. Soon after, my husband met a stranger at a party who, within one month, was instrumental in securing a teaching fellowship for him at a great university.

Imagine my excitement when I heard the university was in England! Tied to a narrow sphere? Within another month, we were crossing the Atlantic and our supposedly insurmountable difficulties melted as though they never existed. We had our year in Europe, one of the happiest years of my life."... M.F.

What the world looks like depends entirely on where man is when he makes his observations. And man, being 'All Imagination,' must be where he is in imagination.

"The stone which the builders rejected has become the chief corner-stone." (*Psalm 118:22*)

That stone is Imagining. I acquaint you with this secret and leave you to Act or Re-act.

> *This is the famous stone*
> *That turneth all to gold:*
> *For that which God doth touch and own*
> *Cannot for less be told.*
>
> –George Herbert "*The Elixir*"

"My home is old but it is mine. I wanted the exterior painted and the interior redecorated, yet I had no money to accomplish either objective. You told us to 'live' as though our desire is already a reality, and this I began to do – imagining my old house with a brand-new coat of paint, new furnishings, new decoration and all the trimmings. I walked, in my imagination, through the newly decorated rooms. I walked around the outside admiring the fresh paint; and, at the end of my imaginal act, I handed the contractor a check for payment in full. I entered this imaginal scene faithfully as often as I could during the day and each night before I fell asleep.

"Within two weeks, I received a registered letter from Lloyd's of London, telling me I had inherited seven thousand dollars from a woman I had never met! I had known her brother slightly almost forty years before and had performed a small service fifteen years ago for the lady when this brother had died in our country, and she had written to me asking for particulars regarding his death which I was able to provide. I had not heard from her since that time.

"Now, here was the check for seven thousand dollars – more than enough to cover the cost of my house restoration, plus many, many other things I desired."... E.C.A.

"He who does not imagine in stronger and better lineaments, and in stronger and better light than his perishing and mortal eye can see, does not imagine at all." – Blake

Unless the individual imagines himself, someone else, or somewhere else, the present conditions and circumstances of his life will continue in being and his problems recur, for all events renew themselves from his constant images. By him they were made; by him they continue in being; and by him they can cease to be.

The secret of causation is in the assembled imagery – but a word of warning – the assemblage must have meaning; it must imply something or it will not form the creative activity – The Word.

CHAPTER 10

Things which do not Appear

"... what is seen was made out of things which do not appear."
–Heb. 11:3

"Human history, with its forms of governments, its revolutions, its wars, and in fact the rise and fall of nations, could be written in terms of the rise and fall of ideas implanted in the minds of men."
–Herbert Hoover

"The secret of imagining is the greatest of all problems to the solution of which the mystic aspires. Supreme power, supreme wisdom, supreme delight lie in the far-off solution of this mystery."
–Douglas Fawcett

To refuse to recognize the creative power of man's invisible, imaginal activity, is too great to be argued with. Man, through his imaginal activity, literally "calls into existence the things that do not exist" (*Romans 4:17*). By man's imaginal activity, all things are made, and without such activity, "was not anything made that was made" (*John 1:3*).

Such causal activity could be defined as, an imaginal assemblage of images, which occurring, some physical event invariably takes place. It is for us to assemble the images of happy outcome and then keep from interfering. The event must not be forced but allowed to happen.

If imagination is the only thing that acts, or is, in existing beings of men (as Blake believed), then "we should never be certain that it was not some woman treading in the wine press who began that subtle change in men's minds" (*William Butler Yeats*).

This grandmother is daily treading the wine press for her little grand-daughter. She writes: "This is one of those things that make my family and friends say, 'we just don't understand it'. Kim is two-and-a-half years old now. I took care of her for a month after she was born and did not see her again until a year ago, and then, only for two weeks. However, during this past year, every day I have taken her on my lap – in my imagination – and cuddled her and talked to her.

"In these imaginal acts, I go over all the wonderful things about Kim: 'God is growing through me; God is loving through me' etc. At first, I would get the response of a very young child. When I started 'God is growing through me' – she would reply, 'Me'. Now – as I start she completes the whole sentence. Another thing that has happened is, as the months have passed, as I take her – in my imagination – on my lap she has grown constantly larger and heavier.

"Kim hasn't even seen a picture of me in this past year. At the most, I could only be a name to her. Now, some time each day, her family tells me, she starts talking about me – to no one in particular – just talking. Sometimes it goes on for an hour; or she goes to the phone and pretends to call. In her monologue are such bits as: 'My Dee Dee loves me. My Dee Dee always comes to see me every day'.

"Even though I know what I have been doing in my imagination, it has caused me, too, 'to wonder much'."... U.K.

All imaginative men and women are forever casting forth enchantments, and all passive men and women, who have no powerful imaginative lives, are continually passing under the spell of their power.

There is no form in nature, which is not produced by, and sustained by some imaginal activity. Therefore, any change in the imaginal activity must result in a corresponding change in form. To imagine a substitute-image for unwanted or defective content is to create it. If only we persist in our ideal imaginal activity and do not let lesser satisfactions suffice, ours shall be the victory.

"When I read in 'Seedtime and Harvest' the story of the school teacher who, through her imagination, in daily revision, transformed a delinquent pupil into a lovely girl, I decided to 'do' something about a young boy in my husband's school.

"To tell all the problems involved would take pages, for my husband has never had such a difficult child nor such a trying parent situation. The lad was too young to be expelled, yet the teachers refused to have him in their classes. To make matters worse, the mother and grandmother literally 'camped' on the school grounds making trouble for everyone.

"I wanted to help the boy, but, I also, wanted to help my husband. So, nightly, I constructed two scenes in my imagination: one, I 'saw' a perfectly normal, happy child; two, I 'heard' my husband say, 'I can't believe it, dear, but do you know "R." is acting like a normal boy, now, and it is heaven not having those two women around'.

"After two months of persisting in my imaginal play, night after night, my husband came home and said, 'It's like heaven around school' – not exactly the same words but close enough for me. The grandmother had become involved in something that took her out of town and the mother had to accompany her.

"At the same time a new teacher had welcomed the challenge of 'R.' and he was progressing wonderfully well into all I imagined for him."... G.B.

It is useless to hold standards that we do not apply. Unlike Portia, who said: "I can easier teach twenty what were good to be done, than be one of the twenty to follow mine own teaching." (William Shakespeare, "*The Merchant of Venice*")

G.B. followed her own teaching. It is fatally easy to make the acceptance of the imaginal faith a substitute for living by it. "... He has sent me to bind up the brokenhearted, to proclaim liberty to the captives, and the opening of the prison to those who are bound..." –Isaiah 61:1

CHAPTER 11

The Potter

"Arise, and go down to the potter's house, and there I will let you hear my words. So, I went down to the potter's house, and there he was working at his wheel. And the vessel he was making of clay was spoiled in the potter's hand, and he reworked it into another vessel, as it seemed good to the potter to do."

–Jeremiah 18:2-4

The word translated 'Potter' means imagination. Out of material others would have thrown away as useless, an awakened imagination refashions it as it ought to be. "O Lord, Thou art our father, we are the clay, and Thou art our potter; we are all the work of Thy hand." Isaiah 64:8

This conception of creation as a work of imagination, and the Lord our Father as our imagination, will take us further into the mystery of creation than any other guide.

The only reason people do not believe in this identity of God and human imagination is that they are unwilling to assume the responsibility for their frightful misuse of imagination.

Divine Imagination has descended to the level of human imagination, that human imagination may ascend to Divine Imagination.

The 8th Psalm says that man was made a little lower than God – not a little lower than the angels – as the King James Version mistakenly translates it. Angels are the emotional dispositions of man and are therefore his servant – and not his superior – as the author of Hebrews tells us. (*Heb. 1:14.*)

Imagination is the Real Man and is one with God.

Imagination creates, conserves and transforms. Imagination is radically creative when all imaginative activity based on memory disappears.

Imagination is conservative when its imaginal activity is fed with images supplied mainly by memory. Imagination is transformative when it varies a theme already in being; when it mentally alters a fact of life; when it leaves the fact out of the remembered experience or puts something in its place if it upsets the harmony it desires.

Through the use of her imagination, this talented young artist has made her dream a reality.

"Ever since I entered into the art field, I have enjoyed doing sketches and paintings for children's rooms. However, I have been discouraged by advisers and friends who were far more experienced in the 'field' than I. They liked my work, admired my talent, but said I would not get recognition nor pay for this type of work.

"Somehow, I always felt I would – but how? Then, last fall I heard your lectures and read your books and I decided to let my imagination create the reality I desired. This is what I did daily: I imagined I was in a gallery – there was a great deal of excitement about me – on the walls hung my 'art' – only mine (*a one-woman show*) – and I saw red stars on many of the pictures. This would indicate that they had been sold.

"This is what happened: Just before Christmas, I did a mobile for a friend who showed it in turn to a friend of hers who owns an art-import shop in Pasadena. He expressed a desire to meet me – so I took a few samples of my work along. When he looked at the very first painting he said he would like to give me 'a one-woman show' in the spring.

"The night of the opening, April 17, an interior decorator came and liked and commissioned me to do a collage for a little boy's room, which will appear in the September issue of Good Housekeeping for the 1961 House of the Year.

"Later, during the showing another decorator came and admired my work so much, he asked if he might arrange for me to meet the 'right' interior decorators and the 'right' owners of galleries who would buy and display my work properly. Incidentally, the show was a financial success for the owner of the gallery, as well as for me.

"The interesting thing about this is that seemingly these three men came to me 'out of the blue'. Certainly, I made no effort during the time of my 'imagining' to contact anyone; but, now, I am getting recognition and have a market for my work. And, now, I know without a shadow of doubt that there is no 'no' when you seriously apply this principle that 'imagining creates reality.'"... G.L.

She tested the Potter and proved His creativity in performance. Only the indolent mind would fail to rise to this challenge. Paul states, "the spirit of God dwells in you" (*1 Cor. 3:16, Romans 8:9, 8:11, James 4:5*), now, "Examine yourselves to see whether you are holding to your faith. Test yourselves. Do you not realize that Jesus Christ is in you? Unless indeed you fail to meet the test! I hope you will find out that we have not failed." 2 Cor. 13:5, 6.

If "all things were made through Him, and without Him was not anything made that was made" (*John 1:3*), it should not be difficult for man to test himself to find out who this creator in himself is. The test will prove to man that his imagination is the One, "who gives life to the dead and calls into existence the things that do not exist." Rom. 4:17

The Potter's presence in us is inferred from what He does there. We cannot see Him there as One, not ourselves. The nature of the Potter – Jesus Christ – is to create and there is no creation without Him.

Every recorded story in this book is just such a test as Paul asked the Corinthians to make. God really and truly exists in man – in every human being. God wholly becomes us. He is not our virtue but our Real Selves – Our Imagination.

The following illustrations from the mineral world may help us to see how Supreme Imagining and Human Imagining could be one and the same power and yet be vastly different in their creativity. Diamond is the world's hardest mineral. Graphite, used in 'lead' pencils, is one of the softest. Yet both minerals are pure carbon. The vast difference in the properties of the two forms of carbon is believed to be caused by a different arrangement of the carbon atoms. But whether the difference is produced by a different arrangement of the carbon atoms or not – all agree that Diamond and Graphite are one substance, pure carbon.

The purpose of life is the creative realization of desire. Man, lacking desire, could not exist efficiently in a world of continuous problems requiring continuing solutions. A desire is an awareness of something we lack or need to make life more enjoyable. Desires always have some personal gain in view. The greater the anticipated gain, the more intense the desire. There is no really unselfish desire. Even when our desire is for another, we are still seeking to gratify desire. To attain our desire we should imagine scenes implying their fulfillment, and enact the scene in our imagination, if only momentarily, with a joy sufficiently felt within its limits to make it natural. It is like a child dressing up and playing "Queen". We must imagine we are what we would like to be. We must play it in imagination first – not as a spectator – as an actor.

This lady imaginatively played "Queen" by being where she wanted to be in her imagination. She was the true actor in this theatre.

"My desire was to attend a matinee performance of a famous pantomimist currently playing in one of the largest theatres of our city. Because of the intimate nature of this art, I wanted to sit in the orchestra; but I didn't have even the price of a balcony ticket. The night I determined to have this pleasure for myself, in my imagination, I fell asleep watching the wondrous performer. In my imaginal act I sat in an orchestra-center seat, heard the applause as the curtain rose and the artist came on stage, and I actually felt the intense excitement of this experience.

"The next day – the day of the matinee performance – my financial condition had not changed. I had exactly one dollar and thirty-seven cents in my purse. I knew I must use the dollar to buy gas for my car which would leave me with thirty-seven cents, but I also knew I had faithfully slept in the feeling of being at that performance, so I dressed myself for the theatre. While changing articles from one purse to another, I found a dollar bill and forty-five cents in change hidden in the pocket of my seldom-used opera purse. I grinned to myself, realizing that gasoline money had been given to me; so would the balance of my theatre ticket be given to me. Gaily I finished dressing and left for the theatre.

"Standing before the ticket window, my confidence dwindled as I gazed at the prices and saw three-seventy-five for orchestra seats. With a feeling of dismay I turned away quickly and walked across the street to a cafe for a cup of tea. I had spent sixteen cents on my tea before I remembered seeing the price of balcony seats on the ticket window list. Hurriedly, I counted my change and found I had one dollar and sixty-six cents left. Running back to the theatre, I bought the cheapest seat available which cost a dollar and fifty-five cents. With one dime left in my purse, I went through the entrance and the usher tore my ticket in half saying, "Upstairs, left, please". The performance was about to begin, but ignoring the usher's instructions, I walked into the main floor lady's restroom. Still determined to sit in the orchestra section, I sat down, closed my eyes and kept my inward 'sight' riveted on the stage from the direction of the orchestra. At that moment, a group of women walked into the restroom, all talking at once, but I heard only one conversation as a woman speaking to her companion, said, 'But I waited and waited until the last moment. Then she called and said she couldn't make it. I would have given her ticket away but it's too late now. Not realizing it, I handed the usher both tickets and he tore them in half before I could stop him'. I almost laughed aloud. Getting up, I walked over to this lady and asked if I might use the extra ticket she had, instead of the balcony seat I had bought. She was charming and kindly invited me to join her party. The ticket she handed me was for the orchestra section, center seat, six rows from the stage.

I sat in that seat only moments before the curtain rose on a performance I had witnessed the night before from that seat – in my Imagination."... J.R.

We must actually BE, in Imagination. It is one thing to think of the end, and another thing to think from the end. To think from the end; to enact the end, is to create reality. The inner actions must correspond to the actions we would physically perform "after these things should be" (Edward Thomas, "*The New House*").

To live wisely, we must be aware of our imaginal activity, and see to it that it is faithfully shaping the end we desire. The world is clay; our Imagination is the Potter. We should always imagine ends that are of value or promise well. "He who desires but acts not breeds pestilence." (*–William Blake*)

What's done flows from what's imagined. Outward forms reveal the imaginings of Man.

"Man is the shuttle, to whose winding quest and passage through these looms God ordered motion, but ordained no rest." (*–Henry Vaughan*)

"I run a small business, solely owned, and a few years ago it seemed that my venture would end in failure. For some months, sales had fallen steadily and I found myself in a financial 'jam' – along with thousands of other small businessmen, as this period spanned one of our country's minor recessions. I was badly in debt and needed at least three thousand dollars almost immediately. My auditors advised me to close my doors and try to salvage what I could. Instead, I turned to my Imagination. I knew your teaching but had never actually attempted to solve any problem in this manner. I was frankly skeptical of the entire idea that imagination can create reality but I was also desperate; and desperation forced me to test your teaching.

"I imagined my office receiving four thousand dollars unexpectedly in remittances due. This money would have to come from new orders as my accounts receivable were practically nonexistent, but this seemed far-fetched as I hadn't received this much in sales during the last four months or more. Nevertheless, I kept my imaginal picture of receiving this amount of money steadily before me for three days. Early the fourth morning a customer I had not heard from in months called me on the telephone asking me to come and see him personally. I was to bring a quotation previously given him for machinery needed by his factory. The quotation was months old, but I dug it out of my files and lost no time in arriving at his office that day. I wrote out the order which he signed, but I saw no immediate help for me in the transaction as the equipment he wanted would take from four to six months for factory delivery, and of course, my customer did not have to pay for it until delivered.

"I thanked him for the order and rose to leave. He stopped me at the door and handed me a check for a little over four thousand dollars, saying, 'I want to pay for the merchandise now, in advance – for tax purposes, you know. You don't mind?' No, I didn't mind. I realized what had happened the moment I took that check into my hands. Within three days, my imaginal act had done for me what I hadn't been able to do in months of desperate financial shuffling. I know, now, that imagination could have brought forty thousand dollars into my business just as easily as four thousands."... L.N.C

> *"O Lord, Thou art our Father; we are the clay, and*
> *Thou art our Potter; we are all the work of Thy hand."*
> –Isaiah 64:8

CHAPTER 12

Attitudes

"Mental Things are alone Real; what is call'd Corporeal, Nobody Knows of its Dwelling Place: it is in Fallacy, and its Existence an Imposture. Where is the Existence Out of Mind or Thought? Where is it but in the Mind of a Fool?"

–Blake

Memory, though faulty, is adequate to the call for sameness. If we remember another as we have known him, we recreate him in that image, and the past will be recognized in the present. Imagining creates reality. If there is room for improvement, we should re-construct him with new content; visualize him as we would like him to be, rather than have him bear the burden of our memory of him. "Everything possible to be believed is an image of truth." (*–Blake*)

The following story is by one who believes that imagining creates reality and acting on this belief changed his attitude toward a stranger and bore witness to this change in reality.

"More than twenty years ago, when I was a 'green' farm boy newly arrived in Boston to attend school, a 'panhandler' asked me for money for a meal. Although the money I had was pitifully insufficient for my own needs, I gave him what was in my pocket. A few hours later the same man, by this time staggering drunk, stopped me again and asked for money. I was so outraged to think the money I could so ill afford had been put to such use, I made myself a solemn pledge that I would never again listen to the plea of a street beggar. Through the years I kept my pledge, but every time I refused anyone, my conscience needled me. I felt guilty even to the point of developing a sharp pain in my stomach, but I couldn't bring myself to unbend.

"The early part of this year, a man stopped me as I was walking my dog and asked for money so he could eat. True to the old pledge, I refused him. His manner was gracious as he accepted my refusal. He even admired my dog and spoke of a family in New York State he knew that raised cocker spaniels. This time my conscience was really pricking me! As he went on his way, I determined to remake that scene as I wished it had been, so I stopped right there on the street, closed my eyes for only a few moments and enacted the scene differently. In my imagination I had the same man approach me, only this time he opened the conversation by admiring my dog. After we had talked a moment, I had him say, 'I don't like to ask you this, but I really need something to eat. I have a job that begins tomorrow morning, but I've been out of work and tonight I'm hungry.' I then reached into my imaginary pocket, pulled out an imaginary five-dollar bill and gladly gave it to him. This imaginal act immediately dissolved the guilty feeling and the pain.

"I know from your teaching that an imaginal act is fact, so I knew I could grant anyone what he asked and by faith in the imaginal act, consent to the reality of his having it.

"Four months later as I was again walking my dog, the same man approached me and opened the conversation by admiring my dog. 'Here's a beautiful dog', he said. 'Young man, I don't suppose you remember me, but awhile back I asked you for some money and you very kindly said "no". I say "kindly", because if you had given it to me I would still be asking for money. Instead, I got a job that very next morning, and now I'm on my feet and have some self-respect again'.

"I knew his job was a fact when I imagined it that night some four months before, but I won't deny there was immense satisfaction in having him appear in the flesh to confirm it!"... F.B.

"I have no silver and gold, but I give you what I have." Acts 3:6.

None is to be discarded, all must be saved, and our Imagination reshaping memory is the process whereby this salvation is brought to pass. To condemn the man for having lost his way is to punish the already punished. "O whom should I pity if I pity not the sinner who is gone astray?" (William Blake, "*Jerusalem*"). Not what the man was, but what he may become should be our imaginal activity.

"Don't you remember sweet Alice, Ben Bolt—
Sweet Alice whose hair was so brown,
Who wept with delight when you gave her a smile,
And trembled with fear at your frown?"

–George Du Maurier

If we imagine no worse of him than he of himself, he would pass as excellent. It's not the man at his best, but the imaginist exercising the spirit of forgiveness that performs the miracle. Imagining with new content transformed both the man who asked and the man who gave. Imagining has not yet had its due in the systems either of moralists or educators. When it does, there will be "the opening of the prison to those who are bound". (*Isa. 61:1*)

Nothing has existence for us save through the memory we have of it, therefore we should remember it not as it was – unless of course, it was altogether desirable – but as we desire it to be.

Inasmuch as imagining is creative, our memory of another either furthers or hinders him, and makes his upward or downward way easier and swifter.

"There is no coal of character so dead that it will not glow and flame if but slightly turned.

"The following story shows that imagining can make rings, and husbands, and move people "to China"!

"My husband, child of a broken home and raised by beloved grandparents, was never 'close' to his mother – nor she to him. A woman of sixty-three and a divorcee for thirty-two of those years, she was lonely and embittered; and my relationship with her was strained as I attempted to 'stay in the middle'. By her own admission, her great desire was to remarry for companionship, but she believed this to be impossible at her age. My husband would often state to me that he hoped she would remarry and, as he fervently put it, 'perhaps live way out of town'!

"I had the same wish and, as I put it, 'perhaps move to China?' Being wary of my personal motive for this wish, I knew I must change my feeling toward her in my imaginal drama and at the same time 'give' her what she wanted. I began by seeing her in my imagination as a completely changed personality – a happy, joyous woman, secure and contented in a new relationship. Every time I thought of her, I would see her mentally as a 'new' woman.

"About three weeks later, she came to our house for a visit bringing a friend she had met many months previously. The man had recently become a widower; he was her age, secure financially and had grown children and grandchildren. We liked him and I was excited because it was obvious they liked each other. But my husband still thought 'it' was impossible. I didn't.

"From that day on, every time her image rose in my mind, I 'saw' her extending her left hand toward me; and I admired the 'ring' on her finger. One month later, she and her friend came to visit us and as I walked forward to greet them, she proudly extended her left hand. The ring was on her finger.

"Two weeks later, she was married – and we haven't seen her since. She lives in a brand-new home... 'way out of town' and as her new husband dislikes the long drive to our house, she might as well have 'moved to China'!"... J.B.

There is a wide difference between the will to resist an activity and the decision to change it. He who changes an activity acts; whereas he who resists an activity, re-acts. One creates; the other perpetuates.

Nothing is real beyond the imaginative patterns we make of it. Memory, no less than desire, resembles a day-dream. Why make it a day-mare? Man can forgive only if he treats memory as a day-dream, and shapes it to his heart's desire.

R.K. learned that we may rob others of their abilities by our attitudes toward them. He changed his attitude and thereby changed a fact.

"I am not a money lender nor am I in the investment business as such, but a friend and business acquaintance came to me for a substantial loan in order to expand his plant. Because of personal friendship, I granted the loan with reasonable interest rates and gave my friend the right of renewal at the end of one year. When the first year term expired, he was behind in his interest payments and requested a thirty-day extension on the note. I granted this request, but at the end of thirty days he was still unable to meet the note and asked for an additional extension.

"As I previously stated, I am not in the business of lending money. Within twenty days, I needed full payment of the loan to meet debts of my own. But I consented again to extend the note although my own credit was now in serious jeopardy. The natural thing to do was to apply legal pressure to collect and a few years ago I would have done just that. Instead, I remembered your warning 'not to rob others of their ability', and I realized that I had been robbing my friend of his ability to pay what he owed.

"For three nights I constructed a scene in my imagination in which I heard my friend tell me that unexpected orders had flooded his desk so rapidly, he was now able to pay the loan in full. The fourth day I received a telephone call from him. He told me that by what he called 'a miracle', he had received so many orders, and big ones, too, he was now able to pay back my loan including all interest due and, in fact, had just mailed a check to me for the entire amount."... R.K.

There is nothing more fundamental to the secret of imagining than the distinction between imagining and the state imagined.

> *"Mental Things are alone Real..."*
> *"Everything possible to be believ'd is an image of truth."*
> –William Blake

CHAPTER 13

All Trivia

"General knowledge is remote knowledge; It is in particulars that wisdom consists. And happiness too."

–Blake

We must use our imagination to achieve particular ends, even if the ends are all trivia. Because men do not clearly define and imagine particular ends the results are uncertain, while they might be perfectly certain. To imagine particular ends is to discriminate clearly. "How do we distinguish the oak from the beech, the horse from the ox, but by the bounding outline?" (*William Blake, Human Form Divine*) Definition asserts the reality of the particular thing against the formless generalizations which flood the mind.

Life on earth is a kindergarten for image making. The bigness or littleness of the object to be created is not in itself important. "The great and golden rule of art, as well as of life", said Blake, "is this: That the more distinct, sharp and wirey the bounding line, the more perfect the work of art, and the less keen and sharp, the greater is the evidence of weak imitation. What is it that builds a house and plants a garden but the definite and determinate?... leave out this line, and you leave out life itself."

The following stories are concerned with the acquiring of seemingly little things, or 'toys' as I call them, but they are important because of the clear imaginal images that created the toys. The author of the first story is one of whom it is said, 'she has everything'. This is true. She has financial, social and intellectual security.

She writes:

"As you know, through your teaching and through my practice of that teaching, I have completely changed myself and my life. Two weeks ago when you spoke of 'toys', I realized I had never used my imagination for the getting of 'things' and I decided it would be fun to try it. You told of a young woman who was given a hat by merely wearing that hat in her imagination. The last thing on earth I needed was a hat, but I wanted to test my imagination for this 'getting of things', so I selected a hat pictured in a fashion magazine. I cut the picture out and stuck it on the mirror of my dressing table. I studied the picture carefully. Then, I shut my eyes, and in my imagination, I put that hat on my head and 'wore' it as I walked out of the house. I did this just once.

"The following week I met some friends for luncheon and one of them was wearing 'the' hat. We all admired it. The very next day, I received a parcel by special delivery messenger. 'The' hat was in the parcel. The friend who had worn it the day before had sent the hat to me with a note saying she did not particularly care for the hat and didn't know why she had bought it in the first place, but for some reason she thought it would look well on me – and would I please accept it!"... G.L.

Movement from 'dreams to things' is the power driving humanity.

We must live wholly on the level of Imagination. And it must be consciously and deliberately undertaken.

"All my life I have loved birds. I enjoy watching them – hearing their chatter – feeding them; and I am particularly fond of the small sparrow. For many months I have fed them crumbs of morning bread, wild bird seed and anything I believed they would eat.

"And for all those months, I have been frustrated as I watched the larger birds – particularly the pigeons – command the area, gobbling up most of the good seed and leaving the husks for my sparrows.

"To use my imagination on this problem seemed facetious to me at first, but the more I thought of it, the more interesting the idea became. So, one night I set about 'seeing' the little birds come in for their full share of daily offerings, and I would 'tell' my wife that the pigeons no longer interfered with my sparrows but took their share like gentlemen and then left the area. I continued this imaginary action for almost one month. Then one morning I noticed that the pigeons had disappeared. The sparrows had breakfast all to themselves for a few days; for those few days no larger bird entered the area. They did return eventually, but to this day they have never again infringed on the area occupied by my sparrows. They stay together, eating what I put out for them, leaving a full share of the area to my tiny friends. And do you know... I actually believe the sparrows understand; they no longer seem to be afraid when I walk among them."... R.K.

This lady proves that unless our heart is in the task, unless we imagine ourselves right into the feeling of our wish fulfilled, we are not there – for we are all imagination, and must be where, and what we are in imagination.

"In early February, my husband and I had been in our new house one month – a home lovely beyond telling, perched on a rugged cliff with the ocean for our front yard, wind and sky for neighbors and seagulls for guests – we were ecstatic. If you have experienced the joy and woe of building your own home, you know how completely filled with happiness you are and how completely empty your purse is: A hundred lovely things clamored to be bought for that house, but the one thing we wanted most of all was the most useless – a picture. Not just any picture, but a wild wonderful scene of the sea dominated by a great white clipper ship. This picture had been in our thoughts all the months of building and we left one living room wall free of paneling to hold it. My husband mounted decorative red and green ship lanterns on the wall to frame our picture, but the picture – itself – would have to wait. Draperies, carpeting – all the practical items must come first. Perhaps so, but that didn't stop either one of us from 'seeing' that picture, in our imagination, on that wall.

"One day, while shopping, I strolled into a small art gallery and as I walked through the door I stopped so suddenly a gentleman walking behind me crashed into an easel. I apologized and pointed to a painting hanging at head-height across the room.

"'That's what did it! I've never seen anything so wonderful!' He introduced himself as the owner of the gallery and said, 'Yes, an original by the greatest English painter of clipper ships the world has known'. He went on to tell me about the artist, but I wasn't listening. I could not take my eyes from that wonderful ship; and suddenly I experienced a very strange thing. It was only a moment in time, but the art gallery faded and I 'saw' that picture on my wall. I'm afraid the owner thought me a little giddy, and I was, but I finally managed to return my attention to his voice when he mentioned an astronomical price. I smiled and said, 'Perhaps some day...' He continued to tell me about the painter and also about an American artist who was the only living lithographer capable of copying the great English master. He said, 'If you're very lucky, you may pick up one of his prints. I've seen his work. It's perfect down to the last detail. Many people prefer prints to paintings.'

"'Prints' or 'paintings', I knew nothing about the values of either, and anyway, all I wanted was that scene. When my husband returned home that evening, I talked of nothing but that painting and pleaded with him to visit the gallery and see it. 'Maybe we could find a print of it somewhere. The man said...' 'Yes', he interrupted, 'but you know we can't afford any picture now...' Our conversation ended there, but that night after dinner, I stood in our living room and 'saw' that picture on our wall.

"The next day, my husband had an appointment with a client which he did not want to keep. But the appointment was kept, and my husband did not return home until after dark. When he walked through the front door, I was busy in another part of the house and called a greeting to him. A few minutes later I heard hammering and walked into the living room to see what he was doing. On our wall hung my picture. In my first moment of intense joy I remembered the man in the art gallery, saying... 'If you're very lucky, you may pick up one of his prints...' Lucky? Well, here is my husband's part of this story:

"Making the call already mentioned, he entered one of the poorest, meanest little houses he had ever been in. The client introduced himself and led my husband into a tiny dark dining area where the two of them sat down at a bare table. As my husband put his brief case on the table top, he looked up and saw the picture on a wall. He confessed to me he had conducted a very sloppy interview because he couldn't take his eyes from that picture. The client signed the contract and gave a check as down payment which, as my husband believed at the time, was ten dollars short. Mentioning this fact to the client, he said the check given was every cent he could afford but added... "I've noticed your interest in that picture. It was here when I took this place. I don't know to whom it belonged, but I don't want it. If you'll put the ten dollars in for me, I'll give you the picture.'

"When my husband returned to his company's main office, he learned he had been in error about the amount. He was not charged ten dollars. Our picture is on our wall. "And it costs us nothing."... A.A.

Of R.L., who writes the following letter, it must be said:

"In faith, Lady, you have a merry heart." (–William Shakespeare, "*Much Ado About Nothing*")

"One day, during a bus strike, I needed to go into the downtown area and had to walk ten blocks from my home to the nearest bus in operation. Before starting home, I recalled there was no food market on this new route and I wouldn't be able to shop for dinner. I had enough to manage a 'pot luck' meal but I would need bread. After shopping all day, the ten blocks back from the bus line was all I could manage and to go still farther to shop for bread was out of the question.

"I stood very still for a moment and allowed a vision of bread to 'dance in my head'. Then I started for home. When I boarded the bus, I was so tired I grabbed the first available seat and almost sat on a paper bag. Now, on a crowded bus tired passengers rarely look directly at one another, so being naturally curious, I peeked into the bag. Of course it was a loaf of bread – not just any bread but the very same brand of bread I always buy!"... R.L.

Trifles: all trifles – but they produced their trivia without price. Imagining accomplished these things without the means generally reputed necessary to do so.

Man rates wealth in a way that bears no relation to real values.

"Come, buy wine and milk without money and without price." –Isaiah 55:1

CHAPTER 14

The Creative Moment

"The natural man does not receive the gifts of the Spirit of God, for they are folly to him, and he is not able to understand them because they are spiritually discerned."

–1 Cor. 2:14.

"There is a Moment in each Day that Satan cannot find, Nor can his Watch Fiends find it; but the Industrious find This Moment & it multiply, & when it once is found It renovates every Moment of the Day if rightly placed."

–Blake

Whenever we imagine things as they ought to be, rather than as they seem to be, is "The Moment". For in that moment, the spiritual man's work is done and all the great events of time start forth to mould a world in harmony with that moment's altered pattern.

Satan, Blake writes, is a "Reactor". He never acts; he only reacts. And if our attitude to the happenings of the day is "reactionary", are we not playing Satan's part?

Man is only reacting in his natural or Satan state; he never acts or creates, he only re-acts or re-creates. One real creative moment, one real feeling of the wish fulfilled, is worth more than the whole natural life of re-action. In such a moment, God's work is done. Once more, we may say with Blake, "God only Acts and Is, in existing beings or Men." (*"The Marriage of Heaven and Hell", 1793*)

There is an imaginal past and an imaginal future. If, by reacting, the past is re-created into the present – so – by acting out our dreams of fancy can the future be brought into the present.

"I feel now the future in the instant." (–William Shakespeare, "*Macbeth*")

The spiritual man Acts: for him, anything that he wants to do, he can do and do at once – in his imagination – and his motto is always, "The Moment is Now".

"Behold, now is the acceptable time; behold, now is the day of salvation." –2 Cor. 6:2

Nothing stands between man and the fulfillment of his dream but facts. And facts are the creations of imagining. If man changes his imagining, he will change the facts.

This story tells of a young woman who found the Moment and, by acting out her dream of fancy, brought the future into the instant, not realizing what she had done until the final scene.

"The incident related below must appear to be coincidence to those never exposed to your teaching – but I know I observed an imaginative act take solid form in, perhaps, four minutes. I believe you will be interested in reading this account, written down, exactly as it happened, a few minutes after the actual occurrence, yesterday morning.

"I was driving my car east on Sunset Boulevard, in the center lane of traffic, braking slowly to stop for a red signal at a three-way intersection, when my attention was caught by the sight of an elderly lady, dressed all in grey, running across the street in front of my car. Her arm was raised, signaling to the driver of a bus which was beginning to pull away from the curb. She was obviously attempting to cross in front of the bus to delay it. The driver slowed his vehicle and I thought would allow her to enter. Instead, as she jumped on to the curb, the bus pulled away leaving her standing just in the act of lowering her arm. She turned and walked swiftly toward a nearby phone booth.

"As my signal changed to green and I put my car in motion, I wished I had been behind the bus and had been able to offer her a ride. Her extreme agitation was obvious even from the distance I was away from her. My wish instantly fulfilled itself in a mental drama, and as I drove away, the fancy played itself out in the following scene..."

I opened the car door and a lady dressed in grey stepped in, smilingly relieved and thanking me profusely. She was out of breath from running and said, 'I only have a few blocks to go. I'm meeting friends and I was so afraid they would leave without me when I missed my bus.' I left my imaginary lady out a few blocks farther on and she was delighted to observe her friends still waiting for her. She thanked me again and walked away..."

"The entire mental scene was spanned in the time it takes to drive one block at a normal rate of speed. The fancy satisfied my feelings regarding the 'real' incident, and I immediately forgot it. Four blocks farther, I was still in the center lane and again had to stop for a red signal. My attention at this time was turned inward on something I have now forgotten, when suddenly someone tapped on the closed window of my car and I looked up to see a lovely-appearing elderly lady with grey hair, dressed all in grey. Smiling, she asked if she might ride a few blocks with me as she had missed her bus. She was out of breath, as though from running, and I was so stunned by her sudden appearance in the middle of a busy street at my window that for a moment I could only react physically, and without answering, leaned over and opened my car door. She got in and said, 'It's so annoying to rush so and then miss a bus. I wouldn't have imposed on you like this, but I'm supposed to meet some friends a few blocks down the street and if I had to walk now, I would miss them.' Six blocks farther on, she exclaimed, 'Oh, good! They're still waiting for me.' I let her out and she thanked me again and walked away.

"I'm afraid I drove to my own destination by automatic reflex, for I had fully recognized that I had just observed a waking dream take form in physical action. I recognized what was happening while it was happening. As soon as I could, I wrote down each part of the incident and found a startling consistency between the 'waking dream' and the subsequent 'reality'. Both women were elderly, gracious in manner, dressed all in grey, and out of breath from hurrying to catch a bus and missing it. Both wished to meet friends (who for some reason could not wait for them much longer) and both left my car within the space of a few blocks after successfully completing their contact with their friends.

"I am amazed, confounded and elated! If there is no such thing as coincidence or accident – then I witnessed imagination become 'reality' almost instantaneously."... J.R.B.

"There is a Moment in each Day that Satan cannot find. Nor can his Watch Fiends find it; but the Industrious find This Moment & it multiply, & when it once is found It renovates every Moment of the Day if rightly placed."

"From the first time I read your 'Search', I have longed to experience a vision. Since you have told us of the 'Promise', this desire has been intensified. I want to tell you of my vision which was a glorious answer to my prayer; but I am sure I would not have had this experience were it not for something that occurred two weeks ago.

"It was necessary for me to park my car some distance from the University Building where I was scheduled to conduct my class. As I left my car, I was conscious of the stillness about me. The street was completely deserted; no one was in sight.

"Suddenly, I heard a most frightful cursing voice. I looked toward the sound and saw a man brandishing a cane, yelling, between vile words, 'I'll kill you. I'll kill you'. I continued on as he approached me, for at that moment I thought 'Now I can test what I have professed to believe; if I do believe we are one, The Father, this derelict and I, no harm can come to me. At that moment I had no fear. Instead of seeing a man coming toward me, I felt a light. He stopped yelling, dropped his cane and walked quietly as we passed with less than a foot between us.

"Having tested my faith at that moment, everything about me had seemed more alive than before – flowers brighter and trees greener. I have had a sense of peace and the 'oneness' of life I had not known before.

"Last Friday, I drove to our country home – nothing was unusual about the day or evening. I worked on a manuscript and, not being tired, did not try to fall off to sleep until around two the following morning. Then I turned off the light and drifted into that floating sensation, not asleep but drowsy, as I call it, half awake and half asleep.

"Often, while in this state – lovely, unknown faces float before me – but this morning the experience was different. A perfect face of a child came before me in profile – then it turned and smiled at me. It was glowing with light and seemed to fill my own head with light.

"I was aglow and excited and thought 'this must be the Christos'; but something within me, without sound, said, 'No, this is you'. I feel I will never be the same again and someday I may experience the 'Promise'."... G.B.

Our dreams will all be realized from the time that we know that Imagining Creates Reality – and Act. But Imagination seeks from us something much deeper and more fundamental than creating things: nothing less indeed than the recognition of its own oneness, with God; that what it does is, in reality, God Himself doing it in and through Man, who is All Imagination.

CHAPTER 15

"The Promise"
Four Mystical Experiences

In all I have related thus far – with the exception of G.B.'s Vision of the Child – imagination was consciously exercised. Men and women created stage plays in their imagination, plays implying the fulfillment of their desires. Then, by imagining themselves participating in these dramas, they created that which their imaginal acts implied. This is the wise use of God's Law. But "No man is justified before God by the Law", Gal. 3:11.

Many people are interested in Imaginism as a way of life, but are not at all interested in its framework of faith, a faith leading to the fulfillment of God's promise. "I will raise up your son after you, who shall come forth from your body... I will be his father, and he shall be My son." 2Sam. 7:12-14

The Promise that God will bring forth from our body a son who will be "born, not of blood nor of the will of the flesh nor of the will of man, but of God" (*John 1:13*) does not concern them.

They want to know God's Law, not His Promise. However, this miraculous birth has been stated clearly as a must for all mankind from the earliest days of the Christian fellowship. "You must be born from above", John. 3:7. My purpose here is to state it again and to state it in such language and with such reference to my own personal mystical experiences that the reader will see that this birth "from above" is far more than a part of a dispensable superstructure, that it is the sole purpose for God's creation.

Specifically, my purpose in recording these four mystical experiences is to show what "Jesus Christ the faithful witness, the firstborn from the dead" (*Rev. 1:5*) was trying to say about this birth from above. "How can men preach unless they are sent?" (*Rom. 10:15*).

Many years ago, I was taken in spirit into a Divine Society, a Society of men in whom God is awake. Though it may seem strange, the gods do truly meet. As I entered this society, the first to greet me was the embodiment of infinite Might. His was a power unknown to mortals. I was then taken to meet infinite Love. He asked me, "What is the greatest thing in the world?" I answered him in the words of Paul, "faith, hope, and love, these three; but the greatest of these is love" (*1 Cor. 13:13*). At that moment, he embraced me and our bodies fused and became one body. I was knit to him and loved him as my own soul. The words, "love of God" so often a mere phrase, were now a reality with a tremendous meaning. Nothing ever imagined by man could be compared with this love which man feels through his union with Love. The most intimate relationship on earth is like living in separate cells compared with this union.

While I was in this state of supreme delight, a voice from outer space shouted, "Down with the blue bloods!" At this blast, I found myself standing before the one who had first greeted me, he who embodied infinite Might. He looked into my eyes and without the use of words or mouth, I heard what he told me: "Time to act". I was suddenly whisked out of that Divine Society and returned to earth. I was tormented by my limitations of understanding but I knew that on that day the Divine Society had chosen me as a companion and sent me to preach Christ – God's promise to man.

My mystical experiences have brought me to accept literally, the saying that all the world's a stage. And to believe that God plays all the parts. The purpose of the play? To transform man, the created, into God, the creator. God loved man, his created, and became man in faith that this act of self-commission would transform man – the created, into God – the creator.

The play begins with the crucifixion of God on man – as man – and ends with the resurrection of man – as God. God becomes as we are, that we may be as He is. God becomes man that man may become, first – a living being, and secondly – a life-giving spirit.

"I have been crucified with Christ; it is no longer I who live, but Christ who lives in me; and the life I now live in the flesh I live by faith in the Son of God, who loved me and gave Himself for me." –Gal. 2:20.

God took upon Himself the form of man and became obedient unto death – even death on the cross of man – and is crucified on Golgotha, the skull of man. God Himself enters death's door – the human skull – and lies down in the grave of man to make man a living being. God's mercy turned death into sleep. Then began the prodigious and unthinkable metamorphosis of man, the transformation of man into God.

No man, unaided by the crucifixion of God, could cross the threshold that admits to conscious life, but now we have union with God in His crucified Self. He lives in us as our wonderful human imagination. "Man is all imagination, and God is man, and exists in us and we in Him. The eternal body of man is the imagination – that is, God, himself" (*Blake*). When He rises in us, we will be like Him and He will be like us. Then all impossibilities will dissolve in us at that touch of exaltation which His rising in us will impart to our nature.

Here is the secret of the world: God died to give man life and to set man free, for however clearly God is aware of His creation, it does not follow that man, imaginatively created, is aware of God. To work this miracle, God had to die, then rise again as man, and none has ever expressed it so clearly as William Blake. Blake says – or rather has Jesus say – "Unless I die, thou canst not live; but if I die I shall arise again and thou with Me. Wouldest thou love one who never died for thee, or ever die for one who had not died for thee? And if God dieth not for man and giveth not Himself eternally for man, man could not exist.

"So God dies – that is to say – God has freely given Himself for man. Deliberately, He has become man and has forgotten that He is God, in the hope that man, thus created, will eventually rise as God. God has so completely offered His own Self for man, that He cries out on the cross of man, "My God, My God; why hast Thou forsaken Me?" (Mat. 27:46; Psalm 21:1). He has completely forgotten that He is God. But after God rises in one man, that man will say to his brothers, "Why stand we here, trembling around, calling on God for help, and not ourselves, in whom God dwells?" (*Blake*)

This first man that has been raised from the dead is known as Jesus Christ – the first fruits of those who have fallen asleep, the first-born of the dead. For man God died; now, by a man, has come also the resurrection of the dead. Jesus Christ resurrects his dead Father by becoming his father. In Adam – the universal man – God sleeps. In Jesus Christ – the individualized God – God wakes. In waking, man, the created, has become God, the creator, and can truly say, "Before the world was, I am" (*Adon Olam, Jewish dogmatics*). Just as God in His love for man so completely identified Himself with man that He forgot that He was God, so man in his love for God must so completely identify himself with God that he lives the life of God, that is, Imaginatively.

God's play which transforms man into God is revealed to us in the Bible. It is completely consistent in imagery and symbolism. The New Testament is hid in the Old Testament, and the old is manifested in the new. The Bible is a vision of God's Law and His Promise. It was never intended to teach history but rather to lead man in faith through the furnaces of affliction to the fulfillment of God's promise, to rouse man from this profound sleep and awaken him as God. Its characters live not in the past but in an imaginative eternity. They are personifications of the eternal spiritual states of the soul. They mark man's journey through eternal death and his awakening to eternal life.

The Old Testament tells us of God's promise. The New Testament tells us not how this promise was fulfilled, but how it is fulfilled. The central theme of the Bible is the direct, individual, mystical experience of the birth of the child, that child of whom the prophet spoke "... to us a child is born, to us a son is given; and the government will be upon his shoulder; and his name will be called, Wonderful Counselor, Mighty God, Everlasting Father, Prince of Peace. Of the increase of his government and of peace, there will be no end..." Isaiah 9:6-7

When the child is revealed to us we see it, we experience it, and the response to this revelation can be stated in the words of Job, "I have heard of thee by the hearing of the ear, but now my eye sees thee" (42:5). The story of the incarnation is not fable, allegory or some carefully contrived fiction to enslave the minds of men, but mystical fact. It is a personal mystical experience of the birth of oneself out of one's own skull, symbolized in the birth of a child, wrapped in swaddling clothes and lying on the floor.

There is a distinction between hearing of this birth of a child from one's own skull – a birth which no scientist or historian could ever possibly explain – and actually experiencing the birth – holding in your own hands and seeing with your own eyes this miraculous child – a child born from above out of your own skull, a birth contrary to all the laws of nature. The question as it is posed in the Old Testament, "Ask now, and see, can a male bear a child? Why then do I see every man with his hands delivering himself like a woman in labor? Why has every face turned pale?" Jer: 30:6. The Hebrew word "chalats", mistranslated "loins", means: to draw out, to deliver, to withdraw self. The drawing of oneself out of one's own skull was exactly what the prophet foresaw as the necessary birth from above, a birth giving man entrance into the kingdom of God and reflective perception on the highest levels of Being. Throughout the ages, "Deep calls to deep" (*Ps. 42:7*); "Rouse thyself! Why sleepest thou, O Lord? Awake!" (*Ps. 44:23*)

The event, as it is recorded in the Gospels, actually takes place in man. But of that day or that hour when the time will come for the individual to be delivered, no one knows but the Father. "Do not marvel that I said to you, You must be born from above. The wind blows where it wills, and you hear the sound of it, but you do not know whence it comes or whither it goes; so it is with everyone who is born of the Spirit." John 3:7-8

This revelation in the Gospel of John is true. Here is my experience of this birth from above. Like Paul, I did not receive it from man – nor was I taught it. It came through the actual mystical experience of being born from above. None can speak truly of this mystical birth from above but one who has experienced it. I had no idea that this birth from above was literally true. Who, before the experience, could believe that the child, the Wonderful Counselor, the Mighty God, the Everlasting Father, the Prince of Peace was in woven in his own skull? Who, before the experience, would understand that his Maker is his Husband and the Lord of Hosts is His Name (*Isaiah 54:5*)? Who would believe that the creator went in unto His own creation, man, and knew it to be Himself and that this entrance into the skull of man – this union of God and man – resulted in the birth of a Son out of the skull of man; which birth gave to that man eternal life and union with his creator forever?

If I now tell what I experienced that night, I do so not to impose my ideas on others, but that I may give hope to those who, like Nicodemus, wonder "how can a man be born when he is old (John 3:4)?" How can he enter a second time into his mother's womb and be born? How can this be? This is how it happened to me. Therefore, I will now "write the vision"; and "make it plain upon tablets, so he may run who reads it. For still the vision awaits its time; it hastens to the end – it will not lie. If it seem slow, wait for it; it will surely come, it will not delay. Behold, he whose soul is not upright in him shall fail, but the righteous shall live by his faith." Hab. 2:2-4.

In the early hours of the morning on July 20, 1959, in the city of San Francisco, a heavenly dream in which the arts flourished was suddenly interrupted by the most intense vibration centered at the base of my skull. Then a drama, as real as those I experience when I am fully awake, began to unfold. I awoke from a dream to find myself completely entombed within my skull. I tried to force my way out through its base. Something gave way and I felt myself move head downward, through the base of my skull. I squeezed myself out, inch by inch. When I was almost out, I held what I took to be the foot of the bed and pulled the remaining portion of me out of my skull. There, on the floor, I lay for a few seconds.

Then I rose and looked at my body on the bed. It was pale of face lying on its back and tossing from side to side like one in recovery from a great ordeal. As I contemplated it, hoping that it would not fall off the bed, I became aware that the vibration which started the whole drama was not only in my head but now was also coming from the corner of the room. As I looked over to that corner, I wondered if that vibration could be caused by a very high wind, a wind strong enough to vibrate the window. I did not realize that the vibration which I still felt within my head was related to that which seemed to be coming from the corner of the room.

Looking back to the bed, I discovered that my body was gone but in its place sat my three older brothers. My oldest brother sat where the head was. My second and third brothers sat where the feet were. None seemed to be aware of me, although I was aware of them and could discern their thoughts. I suddenly became aware of the reality of my own invisibility. I noticed that they, too, were disturbed by the vibration coming from the corner of the room. My third brother was the most disturbed and went over to investigate the cause of the disturbance. His attention was attracted by something on the floor and looking down he announced,

"It's Neville's baby". My other two brothers, in most incredulous voices, asked "How can Neville have a baby?"

My brother lifted the infant wrapped in swaddling clothes and laid him on the bed. I, then, with my invisible hands lifted the babe and asked him "How is my sweetheart?" He looked into my eyes and smiled and I awoke in this world – to ponder this greatest of my many mystical experiences.

Tennyson has a description of Death as a warrior – a skeleton "high on a night-black horse", issuing forth at midnight. But when Gareth's sword cut through the skull, there was in it... "... the bright face of a blooming boy Fresh as a flower new-born." (*Idylls of the King*)

Two other visions I will tell because they bear out the truth of my assertion that the Bible is mystical fact, that everything written about the promised child in the law of Moses and the Prophets and the Psalms must be mystically experienced in the imagination of the individual. The child's birth is a sign and a portent, signaling the resurrection of David, the Lord's anointed, of whom He said, "You are My Son, today I have begotten You", Psalms 2:7.

Five months after the birth of the child, on the morning of December 6, 1959, in the city of Los Angeles, a vibration similar to the one which preceded his birth started in my head. This time its intensity was centered at the top of my head. Then came a sudden explosion and I found myself in a modestly furnished room. There, leaning against the side of an open door was my son David of Biblical fame. He was a lad in his early teens. What struck me forcibly about him was the unusual beauty of his face and figure. He was – as he is described in the first book of Samuel – ruddy, with beautiful eyes and very handsome (*16:12, 17:42*).

Not for one moment did I feel myself to be anyone other than who I am now. Yet, I knew that this lad, David, was my son, and he knew that I was his father; for "the wisdom from above is without uncertainty" (But the wisdom that is from above is first pure, then peaceable, gentle, and easy to be intreated, full of mercy and good fruits, without partiality, and without hypocrisy, James 3:17). As I sat there contemplating the beauty of my son, the vision faded and I awoke.

"I and the children whom the Lord has given me are signs and portents in Israel from the Lord of hosts, who dwells on Mount Zion", Is. 8:18. God gave me David as my very own son. "I will raise up your son after you, who shall come forth from your body... I will be his father, and he shall be my son", 2Sam. 7:12-14. God is known in no other way than through the Son.

"No one knows who the Son is, except the Father, or who the Father is, except the Son and any one to whom the Son chooses to reveal Him", Luke. 10:22. The experience of being David's Father is the end of man's pilgrimage on earth. The purpose of life is to find the Father of David, the Lord's anointed, the Christ. 'Abner, whose son is this youth?' And Abner said, 'As your soul lives, O king, I cannot tell.' And the king said, 'Inquire whose son the stripling is.' And as David returned from the slaughter of the Philistine, Abner took him and brought him before Saul with the head of the Philistine in his hand. And Saul said to him, 'Whose son are you, young man?' And David answered, 'I am the son of your servant Jesse the Bethlehemite', 1 Sam. 17:55-58. Jesse is any form of the verb 'to be'. In other words, I Am the Son of who I Am, I am self begotten, I Am the Son of God, the Father. I and My Father are one (John 10:30). I am the image of the invisible God. He who has seen Me has seen the Father (*John 14:9*).

'Whose son...?' is not about David, but about David's Father, whom the king had promised (*1 Sam. 17:25*) to make free in Israel. Note: in all these passages (*1 Sam. 17:55, 56, 58*) the king's inquiry is not about David but about David's Father.

'I have found David, my servant... He shall cry to Me, "Thou art my Father, my God, and the Rock of my salvation. And I will make him the first-born, the highest of the kings of the earth", Psalm 89 (:20; 26-27).

The individual who is born from above will find David and know him to be his very own son. Then he will ask the Pharisees – who are always with us – "What do you think of the Christ? Whose son is He?" And when they say to him, "The son of David", he will say to them, "How is it then that David, in the Spirit, calls him Lord... If David thus calls him Lord, how is he his son?" Matt: 22:41-45. Man's misconception of the role of the Son – which is only a sign and a portent – has made the Son an idol. "Little children, keep yourselves from idols." 1 John 5:21.

God awakes; and that man in whom he awakes becomes his own father's father. He who was David's Son, "Jesus Christ, the son of David" Matt. 1:1 has become David's Father.

No longer will I cry to "our father David, thy child", Acts. 4:25. "I have found David" (*Psalm 89:20, Acts 13:22*). He has cried to me, "Thou art my Father", Ps. 89 (:26). Now I know myself to be one of the Elohim, the God who became man, that man may become God. "Great indeed, we confess, is the mystery of our religion", 1 Tim. 3:16. If the Bible were history, it would not be a mystery. "Wait for the promise of the Father", Acts. 1:4, that is, for David – God's Son – who will reveal you as the Father. This promise, says Jesus, you heard from Me (*Luke 24:44*) and to its fulfillment at that moment in time when it pleases God to give you His Son – as "your offspring, which is Christ", Gal. 3:16.

A figure of speech is used for the purpose of calling attention to, emphasizing and intensifying the reality of the literal sense. The truth is literal; the words used are figurative. "The curtain of the temple was torn in two, from top to bottom, and the earth shook and the rocks were split", Matt. 27:51.

On the morning of April 8, 1960 – four months after it was revealed to me that I am David's father – a bolt of lightning out of my skull split me in two from the top of my skull to the base of my spine. I was cleft as though I were a tree that had been struck by lightning. Then I felt and saw myself as a golden liquid light moving up my spine in a serpentine motion; as I entered my skull, it vibrated like an earthquake. "Every word of God proves true; he is a shield to those who take refuge in him. Do not add to his words, lest he rebuke you, and you be found a liar" (*Proverbs 30:5, 6*). "And as Moses lifted up the serpent in the wilderness, so must the Son of man be lifted up", John 3:14.

These mystical experiences will help to rescue the Bible from the externals of history, persons and events, and to restore it to its real significance in the life of man. Scripture must be fulfilled "in" us. God's promise will be fulfilled. You will have these experiences: "And you shall be my witnesses in Jerusalem and in all Judea and Sa-ma-ri-a land to the end of the earth", Acts 1:8.

The widening circle – Jerusalem... Judea... Samaria, the end of the earth – is God's plan.

The Promise is still maturing to its time, its appointed time, but how long, vast and severe the trials e're you find David, your son, who will reveal you as God, The Father, were long to tell;

but it hastens to the end; it will not fail. So wait, for there will be no postponement.

"Is anything too wonderful for the Lord? At the appointed time I will return to you, in the spring, and Sarah shall have a son", Gen. 18:14.

OTHER BOOKS YOU MAY LIKE

- 1984 by George Orwell, ISBN: 9789380914947
- 12 Years a Slave by Solomon Northup, ISBN: 9789390492374
- 51 Most Powerful Prayers by Ryan, ISBN: 9789354990847
- A Christmas Carol by Charles Dickens, ISBN: 9788193545874
- A Cloud by Day, a Fire by Night by AW Tozer, ISBN: 9789354990854
- A Passage to India by E.M. Forster, ISBN: 9789354990205
- A Room of One's Own by Virginia Woolf, ISBN: 9789354990281
- A Streetcar Named Desire by Tennessee Williams, ISBN: 9788194748601
- A Wrinkle in Time by Madeleine L'Engle, ISBN: 9789354991066
- Abraham Lincoln by Lord Charnwood, ISBN: 9789380914251
- Absolute Surrender by Andrew Murray, ISBN: 9789389716269
- Animal Farm by George Orwell, ISBN: 9789380914701
- Anthem by Ayn Rand, ISBN: 9789389157079
- As a Man Thinketh by James Allen, ISBN: 9788180320262
- As I Lay Dying by William Faulkner, ISBN: 9789390492381
- Awakened Imagination by Neville Goddard, ISBN: 9789389157086
- Be What You Wish by Neville Goddard, ISBN: 9789387669550
- Chanakya Neeti by Chanakya, ISBN: 9789389716276
- Civilization and Its Discontents by Sigmund Freud, ISBN: 9789387669499
- Delighting in God by AW Tozer, ISBN: 9788194748632
- Demian by Hermann Hesse, ISBN: 9789387669567
- Experiencing the Holy Spirit by Andrew Murray, ISBN: 9788194764809
- Feeling is the Secret by Neville Goddard, ISBN: 9789389157109
- George Orwell Combo : Animal Farm & 1984, ISBN: 9789390492459
- Gravity by George Gamow, ISBN: 9789388118484
- Guerrilla Warfare by Ernesto Che Guevara, ISBN: 9789354990366

Develop your reading habit | **Gift books to your friends**

OTHER BOOKS YOU MAY LIKE

- How to be filled with the Holy Spirit by AW Tozer, ISBN: 9789389157116
- How to Develop Self Confidence by Dale Carnegie, ISBN: 9789387669000
- In His Steps by Charles M. Sheldon, ISBN: 9789390492794
- Life of Christ by Fulton J. Sheen, ISBN: 9789389716306
- Lost Horizon by James Hilton, ISBN: 9789389716313
- Man: The Dwelling Place of God by AW Tozer, ISBN: 9789354990656
- Maneaters of Kumaon by Jim Corbett, ISBN: 9789354990731
- Mansarover 1 (Hindi) by Premchand, ISBN: 9789380914978
- Mansarover 2 (Hindi) by Premchand, ISBN: 9789380914985
- Meditation and Its Methods by Swami Vivekananda, ISBN: 9789389716320
- One, None and a Hundred Thousand by Luigi Pirandello, ISBN: 9789389716337
- Paths to Power by AW Tozer, ISBN: Forthcoming
- Scientific Healing Affirmations by P. Yogananda, ISBN: 9789389716344
- Selected Stories of Rabindranath Tagore by Tagore, ISBN: 9789380914770
- Siddhartha by Hermann Hesse, ISBN: 9789380914145
- Student's Encyclopedia of G. K. by GP Editors, ISBN: 9789380914190
- Tales from Shakespeare by Charles Lamb & Mary Lamb, ISBN: 9789380914367
- The Alchemy of Happiness by Al-Ghazzali, ISBN: 9789387669505
- The Book of Enoch by Enoch, ISBN: 9789390492480
- The Dynamic Laws of Prosperity by Catherine Ponder, ISBN: 9789388118156
- The Game of Life and How to Play It by Florence Shinn, ISBN: 9789387669390
- The Imitation of Christ by Thomas À Kempis, ISBN: 9789388118057
- The Knowledge of the Holy by AW Tozer, ISBN: 9789389157130
- The Law by Neville Goddard, ISBN: 9789390492886
- The Light of Asia by Sir Edwin Arnold, ISBN: 9789380914923
- The Magic of Believing by Claudie Bristol, ISBN: 9789388118149

Develop your reading habit | **Gift books to your friends**

OTHER BOOKS YOU MAY LIKE

- The Magic of Faith by Joseph Murphy, ISBN: 9789388118743
- The Miracles of Your Mind by Joseph Murphy, ISBN: 9788180320743
- The Mysterious Affair at Styles by Agatha Christie, ISBN: 9789390492510
- The Origin of Species by Charles Darwin, ISBN: 9788180320453
- The Plague by Albert Camus, ISBN: 9788194764892
- The Power of Awareness by Neville Goddard, ISBN: 9789387669406
- The Power of Positive Thinking by Norman Vincent Peale, ISBN: 9789388118569
- The Problem of Increasing Human Energy by Nikola Tesla, ISBN: 9789354990953
- The Prophet by Kahlil Gibran, ISBN: 9789380914022
- The Psychopathology of Everyday Life by Sigmund Freud, ISBN: 9789388118071
- The Pursuit of God by AW Tozer, ISBN: 9789389157147
- The Railway Children by E Nesbit, ISBN: 9789354990960
- The Red Badge of Courage by Stephen Crane, ISBN: 9789354990977
- The Sound and the Fury by William Faulkner, ISBN: 9789390492572
- The Stranger by Albert Camus, ISBN: 9789390492589
- The Sun Also Rises by Ernest Hemingway, ISBN: 9789354990984
- The Yoga Sutras of Patanjali by Patanjali, ISBN: 9789389716351
- Their Eyes Were Watching God by Zora Neale Hurston, ISBN: 9788194764885
- Think and Grow Rich by Napoleon Hill, ISBN: 9788180320255
- Thought Vibration by William Walker Atkinson, ISBN: 9789389157154
- To the Lighthouse by Virginia Woolf, ISBN: 9789390492190
- Who were the Shudras by Dr B.R. Ambedkar, ISBN: 9789354991028
- World's Best Short Stories: Volume 1 by Various Authors, ISBN: 9789390492275
- Wuthering Heights by Emily Brontë, ISBN: 9788193545898
- Your Faith is Your Fortune by Neville Goddard, ISBN: 9789389157161
- Zen in the Art of Archery by Eugen Herrigel, ISBN: 9789354991059

Develop your reading habit | **Gift books to your friends**

www.ingramcontent.com/pod-product-compliance
Ingram Content Group UK Ltd.
Pitfield, Milton Keynes, MK11 3LW, UK
UKHW040229300826
14791UKWH00001B/70

9 789354 994586